ENTERTAINING SOLO

Also by Claire Macdonald

Seasonal Cooking

The Harrods Book of Entertaining

Delicious Fish

More Seasonal Cooking

Celebrations

Suppers

Sweet Things

The Best of Food and Drink in Scotland

Lunches

The Claire Macdonald Cookbook

Simply Seasonal

Claire Macdonald's

delicious recipes for single cooks who like to entertain

ENTERTAINING SOLO

BANTAM PRESS

LONDON · NEW YORK · TORONTO · SYDNEY · AUCKLAND

TRANSWORLD PUBLISHERS
61–63 Uxbridge Road, London W5 5SA
a division of The Random House Group Ltd

RANDOM HOUSE AUSTRALIA (PTY) LTD
20 Alfred Street, Milsons Point, Sydney,
New South Wales 2061, Australia

RANDOM HOUSE NEW ZEALAND LTD
18 Poland Road, Glenfield, Auckland 10, New Zealand

RANDOM HOUSE SOUTH AFRICA (PTY) LTD
Endulini, 5a Jubilee Road, Parktown 2193, South Africa

Published 2002 by Bantam Press
a division of Transworld Publishers

Copyright © Claire Macdonald 2002

Illustrations © Beverly Levy 2002
Photography © Jean Cazals 2002
Home economist: Marie-Ange Lapierre

A catalogue record for this book is available from the British Library.
ISBN 0593 050223

Typeset in Univers by Falcon Oast Graphic Art Ltd

Printed in Great Britain

10 9 8 7 6 5 4 3 2 1

For Godfrey
Alexandra and Philipp
Isabella and Tom
Meriel and Sebastian
and Hugo

Acknowledgements

My entire life consists of two things: family and food. I have dedicated this book to the first, and as to the second – well, there are four people above all others with whom I share the food side of my life. My dear friend Araminta Dallmeyer – Minty and I do pretty well all my cooking demonstrations together, and much else besides; and Peter Macpherson, Kath Stephenson and Jenny Aldridge, here in the kitchen at Kinloch, who are unfailingly patient and tolerant with my culinary ideas and inspirations, and who cook so very well themselves that they are chiefly responsible for the great number of our guests who return again and again.

My sister Olivia Milburn and my cousin Judith Coleridge are not only two of my dearest friends but also those with whom I discuss endless culinary matters – they and I are of such like minds. I'm indebted to Maggie Pearlstine, Nicki Harris and John Oates – I count each one as my agent and friend.

And Sally Gaminara, who has been such a part of my life for so long – I'm so grateful to her. But new to me this book is Mari Roberts, and I am extremely grateful to her for all her help with the editing.

And a big thank-you, too, to Julia Lloyd, who is, simply, the best of designers – I love the cover of this book and all the graphics within.

Contents

Introduction

Several years ago I was visited by a retired friend who had led a very busy and sociable professional life, and whose life in retirement seemed no less busy and certainly every bit as sociable. She asked me if I would think of writing a book for people like her: could I imagine what it was like to entertain single-handed? I thought of how flustered I would be if I had to answer the door, take coats, pour drinks and attend to last-minute details in the kitchen. So, here is a book that I hope will answer the needs of many who live alone in Britain – apparently over 40 per cent of the population.

Virtually all of the recipes can be made ahead, either in entirety or to a great degree, and few need last-minute attention. In many cases the main course consists of one dish: single-handed entertaining continues after your guests have left – or, if they are staying, gone to bed. Nothing is more bleak than clearing up the aftermath of a party on your own. Don't forget that baking parchment in a roasting or baking tray saves endless soaking and scrubbing later. And offer one type of drink before lunch or dinner – it saves having to provide sliced lemon or lime, ice, mixers and assorted glasses. Champagne or any sparkling white wine is perfect.

But, of course, you don't have to live alone to find this book useful! I hope its contents will ease the path of many cooks, whether or not they are entertaining solo.

First and li

ght courses

In this chapter you will find recipes for all types of first courses. There are thin, elegant soups, such as the Roast Red Pepper and Celery Soup (page 51), or thick, hearty Ham and Butterbean Vegetable Soup (page 53), which makes a meal in itself. I was inspired to make Potato Soup with Crispy Bacon Bits (page 54) after a visit to our daughter, who lives in Austria. The creamy Brussels Sprout and Chestnut Soup (page 55) is enhanced by a dash of balsamic vinegar.

If you increase the quantities many of the recipes in this chapter make excellent main courses – Mushroom Strudel on page 20, perhaps. Chicken and Avocado Terrine (page 40) lends itself well to a light lunch, as does the Warm Chicken Liver Salad with Fried Walnut Dressing (page 36).

Some dishes are served cold, and others hot, or warm. The Cheese and Pecan Profiteroles (page 14) can be served either warm or cold, as can Red Onion Cream Tart with Walnut and Parmesan Pastry (page 26). Most of the soups are eaten hot, while the Roast Aubergine Mousse with Tomato, Black Olive and Caper Relish (page 32) is cold, as is the Blue Cheese Mousse (page 28). Convenience to the cook is a quality all of the recipes share – but not at the expense of taste!

Cheese and pecan profiteroles

filled with herb and garlic cream cheese

These are especially good for those who do not include meat or fish in their diet. The profiteroles can be made a day in advance and kept in an airtight container, and the pecans add a lovely contrasting crunch. The filling takes seconds to whiz together in a food processor; you can make it a day ahead too, then keep it in the fridge until you are ready to fill the profiteroles, which you can do on the day, up to 6 hours ahead. If you like, put the filled profiteroles into a low-temperature oven for 30–45 minutes to serve them warm, but they are just as good cold. This recipe allows 2 profiteroles per person, with maybe a couple over.

Serves 6

8 oz/225 g plain flour

1 rounded tsp mustard powder

1 pint/450 ml water

6 oz/175 g butter, diced

4 oz/110 g strong Cheddar cheese, grated

4 large eggs, beaten well together

3 oz/75 g pecans, chopped and dry-fried for several minutes

for the filling

2 fat cloves of garlic, skinned

2 tsp salt

1 lb/450 g cream cheese, such as Philadelphia

1 tbsp chopped parsley

1 tbsp snipped chives

a pinch of paprika

First make the profiteroles. Preheat the oven to 420°F/220°C/Gas Mark 7.

Sieve the flour twice with the mustard powder. Pour the water into a saucepan and add the butter, then let it melt over a moderate heat. Then bring the liquid to a rolling boil. Add the twice-sieved flour and mustard powder in a whoosh, and beat well. When the flour is all incorporated, take the pan off the heat, and continue to beat until the dough rolls away from the sides of the saucepan. Beat in the cheese, and the eggs, a little at a time, until you have a smooth, glossy dough. This can be quite hard work, so use a hand-held electric beater rather than a wooden spoon if you have one. Lastly beat in the pecan nuts.

You cannot pipe this mixture because the chopped nuts will stick in the nozzle of your piping bag, so, take 2 teaspoons, and dip them in cold water. Dampen 2 baking sheets with water. Using the 2 spoons, make even-sized blobs, about the size of a ping-pong ball, of the dough and place on the baking sheets. Put them into the hot oven (top right oven in a 4-door Aga) for 15–20 minutes – when they are ready, they should be firm and dark golden. Swap around the baking trays just before the end of cooking (because no oven ever cooks evenly). Remove the profiteroles from the baking trays with a palette knife and let them cool on a wire rack. When they are cold, store them in an airtight container.

On the day of serving, make the filling. Pulp the garlic and the salt, then beat it with all of the other ingredients until everything is thoroughly mixed. Cover and keep in a cool place.

· ·

To serve, cut each profiterole nearly in half, widthways, and divide the filling between them. If you like, serve them with a small amount of vinaigrette-dressed salad leaves.

Chive crêpes with creamy spinach and cumin filling

and tomato and chilli sauce

The crêpes can be made ahead, and frozen, but make sure you steam all the excess liquid from the spinach as it cooks. They will take 2½–3 hours to thaw at room temperature. The sauce, too, freezes well. Otherwise you can make and fill the crêpes a day in advance and keep them in the fridge.

Serves 6

for the crêpes
2 large eggs
4 oz/110 g plain flour
½ pint/300 ml milk + 2 tbsp cold water
2 tbsp snipped chives
½ tsp salt
a good grinding of black pepper
a grating of nutmeg
2 oz/50 g butter, for frying

for the filling
3 tbsp olive oil
2 onions, skinned and chopped
1 rounded tsp cumin seeds
1¼ lb/675 g fresh baby spinach
1–2 cloves of garlic, to taste, skinned and chopped
½ tsp salt
a good grinding of black pepper
1 lb/450 g cream cheese, such as Philadelphia

for the sauce
3 tbsp olive oil
2 onions, skinned and chopped
1 clove of garlic, skinned and chopped
2 sticks celery, washed and trimmed
2 x 15 oz/400 g cans chopped tomatoes
½ tsp salt
a good grinding of black pepper
½ tsp sugar
½ tsp dried chilli flakes

first and light courses

To make the crêpes put all the ingredients, except the butter, into a blender and whiz. Leave the batter to rest for at least 1 hour before you make the crêpes. Melt the butter in a non-stick crêpe pan (or small frying pan). Stir the batter, then, when the butter is foaming, pour in a small amount of batter (about 2 tablespoons), tipping and tilting the pan until the bottom is evenly coated. Cook for a few seconds, then flip it over, using your thumbs fleetingly to loosen it and help it over if you like. Cook for a few seconds on the other side, then slide the cooked crêpe on to a plastic tray to cool. If you have to use a wooden board for this, cover it with a cloth or the crêpes will stick to it. Continue, adding butter to the pan as you need it, until all of the batter has been used. You should end up with 12 crêpes. Stack them only when they are cold and cover them with a cloth.

For the filling, heat the oil in a large sauté pan, put in the onions and the cumin then cook until the onions are transparent and just turning golden. Meanwhile, steam the spinach – it may look a vast amount when fresh, but it wilts down to very little. Stir the steamed spinach into the onions and cumin, then add the garlic. Season with salt and pepper, let it cool a little then put it into a food-processor with the cream cheese and whiz. Scrape the mixture into a bowl.

To fill the crêpes, lay them flat on a work surface, and divide the filling between them: spoon it into a mound in the middle of each. Fold the sides over, to form a flat parcel. Rub an ovenproof dish with olive oil, and put the filled crêpes into it. Brush each with olive oil, cover them with clingfilm, then either freeze, or store them in the fridge until you are ready to heat them.

To make the sauce, heat the oil in a saucepan and add the onions, garlic and celery. Cook over a moderate heat until the onion is soft and transparent, then add the tomatoes, the salt, pepper, sugar and chilli. Stir well, then simmer for 10–15 minutes. Let the mixture cool, then liquidize it and pour the velvety smooth sauce into a clean saucepan to reheat as required.

. . . .

To reheat the crêpes preheat the oven to 350°F/180°C/Gas Mark 4. Leave the crêpes at room temperature for 30 minutes before you put them into the moderate oven (bottom right oven in a 4-door Aga) for 20–25 minutes. Serve with the reheated sauce on the side and, if you like, a salad of mixed leaves and some warm bread.

Herb crêpes with wild mushrooms

and white truffle cream sauce

This is a rather rich first course (in larger quantities it makes a good main course) so follow it with a fairly light main course – try the Baked Sea Bass with Lemon-and-thyme-dressed Beans and Tomatoes on page 78. You can prepare the batter 2 days in advance, but the crêpes should be made and filled only a day ahead. Unlike the Chive Crêpes on page 16, they don't freeze well. The white truffle paste in the cream sauce is available from many delicatessens and some good supermarkets.

Serves 6

for the crêpes
2 large eggs
4 oz/110 g plain flour
½ pint/300 ml milk + 2 tbsp cold water
2 tbsp chopped mixed herbs, such as flat-leaf parsley and snipped chives,
with a little thyme, chervil or dill
½ tsp salt
a good grinding of black pepper
a grating of nutmeg
2–3 oz/50–75 g butter, for frying

for the filling
1½ lb/675 g assorted wild mushrooms such as chanterelles, horns-of-plenty,
oyster, or shiitake, cleaned and evenly chopped
4 tbsp olive oil
½ tsp thyme leaves
1 tsp salt

for the white truffle cream sauce
1 jar La Truffata white truffle paste
¾ pint/450 ml double cream
a good grinding of black pepper
a pinch of salt

Put all the crêpe ingredients, except the butter, into a blender and whiz. Leave the batter to rest for at least 30 minutes. To make the crêpes, melt a little butter in a non-stick crêpe pan (or small frying pan). Stir the batter, and, when the butter is foaming, pour a small amount of batter (about 2 tablespoons) into the pan, tipping and

first and light courses

tilting so that the base is evenly coated. Cook for a few seconds and then with the fleeting help of thumbs – *I* need to use my thumbs – flip it over, then cook for a few seconds on the other side. Lay the cooked crêpe on a plastic tray to cool before stacking. Continue, adding more butter as you need it, until all the butter has been used. You should end up with 12 crêpes.

To make the filling, preheat the oven to 400°F/200°C/Gas 6. Line a baking tray with baking parchment and lay on it the mushrooms. With your hands, mix into them the olive oil, thyme, and salt. Put them into the hot oven (top right oven in a 4-door Aga) for 20 minutes, then shuffle them around on the baking tray and put the tin back for a further 15–20 minutes. Let the mushrooms cool, then divide them between the crêpes. Roll the crêpes into a cigar shape, and lay them side by side in a buttered or oiled ovenproof dish.

To make the sauce, put all of the ingredients into a saucepan and simmer for a couple of minutes. Then pour the sauce over the rolled-up crêpes. Cover the dish with baking parchment, and store them in the fridge until 30 minutes before you need to reheat them.

· ·

Take the crêpes out and let them come to room temperature. Bake in a preheated moderate oven, 350°F/180°C/Gas Mark 4 (bottom right oven in a 4-door Aga), for 20–25 minutes. Serve warm or hot.

Mushroom strudel

with white truffle cream sauce

This can be prepared several hours in advance up to the baking stage – in the morning, for that evening, perhaps. It doesn't really need a sauce, but the White Truffle Cream Sauce (see page 18) complements it well and also acts as a garnish. You can use wild mushrooms instead of flat field mushrooms, if you prefer and depending on the time of year.

Serves 6

4 sheets filo pastry
3 oz/75 g butter, melted

for the filling
3 oz/75 g fresh white *or* brown bread
a large handful of parsley
1½ lb/675 g field mushrooms, wiped and chopped
4 tbsp olive oil
2 oz/50 g butter
1 tsp salt
1 onion, skinned and very finely chopped
1–2 cloves of garlic, to taste, skinned and very finely chopped
a good grinding of black pepper
a grating of nutmeg
½ pint/300 ml double cream
1 tbsp lemon juice

white truffle cream sauce (see page 18)

Preheat the oven to 420°F/220°C/Gas Mark 7. Put the bread into the food-processor with the parsley and whiz until you have green-flecked crumbs. Line a baking tray with a sheet of baking parchment. Lay the chopped mushrooms on it and, with your fingers, mix in the 3 tablespoons of olive oil. Put the tray into the hot oven (top right oven in a 4-door Aga) for 20 minutes, then shuffle the mushrooms around and roast for a further 10–15 minutes. Take them out and let them cool. Meanwhile, in a large sauté pan, melt the butter, add the salt, and when the butter is foaming fry the parsley breadcrumbs in it, stirring, until they are golden brown and crisp. Scoop them on to a warmed dish. Wipe out the pan with kitchen roll. Heat the remaining tablespoon of olive oil in the same pan and sauté the onion until it is soft and transparent and beginning to turn golden. Then add the garlic, and continue to cook for a further minute. Now stir in the roast mushrooms and season with pepper and nutmeg. Pour in the cream and lemon juice, and stir until the sauce bubbles and thickens. Take the pan off the heat and let it cool. Then mix in the parsley crumbs.

Lay a sheet of filo on a work surface and brush it thoroughly with melted butter. Carefully cover it with a second sheet of filo, and brush it with melted butter. Put half of the mushroom mixture in a line down the middle, fold either side up and over, and crimp it together in the middle. Repeat with the other 2 sheets of filo. Brush a roasting tin with melted butter, and carefully put into it the two strudels, join side down. Brush both with melted butter. (If you do this in advance, cover them with clingfilm to prevent them drying out.) Store in the fridge for several hours but restore to room temperature for half an hour before putting them in the oven. Remove the clingfilm before you bake them.

· ·

Put the tin into a preheated hot oven, 400°F/200°C/Gas Mark 6 (top right oven in a 4-door Aga), for 20–25 minutes until the strudels are a deep golden brown. Serve warm, sliced thickly, with a spoonful of the reheated white truffle cream sauce.

Crab, garlic and cream cheese filo triangles

These can be prepared in the morning, ready to bake for supper or dinner. Serve them warm, not hot – they are easier to eat and the flavours seem better. If you don't like garlic, leave it out. This recipe makes 2 large triangles per person. I don't think they need a sauce but if you would like one, the simplest is best: just simmer ¾ pint/450 ml double cream with 2 teaspoons of lemon juice, a pinch of salt and a good grinding of black pepper for 3 minutes. Stir in 2 tablespoons of snipped chives and serve it warm.

Serves 6

4 sheets filo pastry
4 oz/110 g butter, melted

for the filling **8 oz/225 g cream cheese, such as Philadelphia**
1 clove of garlic, skinned and finely chopped
1 tsp Tabasco
2 tsp salt
a good grinding of black pepper
1 lb/450 g best quality crabmeat, mixed white and brown meat
1 tbsp chopped parsley, preferably flat-leaf

First make the filling. Put the cream cheese into a food-processor and whiz it with the garlic, Tabasco, salt and pepper. Then whiz in the crabmeat and parsley. Scrape it into a bowl.

Butter 1 large or 2 smaller baking trays. Lay a rectangle of filo on a work surface and brush it thoroughly with melted butter. Carefully cover it with a second sheet of filo, and brush it, too, with melted butter. Cut it into 3 wide strips, then cut across each, to give you 6 shorter strips. Put a spoonful of the crab mixture in the bottom left corner of each strip. Draw the right-hand corner diagonally across to form a triangle. Fold the triangle over at its base and then continue folding up the strip until the parcel is complete. Put the triangle on to the baking tray, and brush it with more melted butter. Repeat with the remaining 2 sheets of filo. Store them, covered, in the fridge until 30 minutes before you need to cook them.

first and light courses

. . . .

Take the filo triangles out of the fridge, let them come to room temperature, and bake them in a preheated hot oven, 420°F/220°C/ Gas Mark 7 (top right oven in a 4-door Aga), for 10 minutes or until they are a deep golden brown. Meanwhile, make a simple sauce (see introduction) if desired. Serve the triangles freshly baked and still warm.

Potted smoked trout

with horseradish and lemon

Serves 6

This is such a convenient first course. It can be made up to two days in advance, providing that you clingfilm each ramekin once the clarified butter has set to prevent the air in the fridge drying the butter, which will then crack. Horseradish and lemon enhance the taste of the smoked trout. For me, the best horseradish cream is that made by Moniack. Avoid anything harshly vinegared; it would spoil the dish. I like to serve Melba toast with this.

6 x 2–3 oz/50–75 g fillets of hot-smoked trout
1 tbsp chopped flat-leaf parsley
3 tsp best horseradish cream (see introduction, above)
plenty of black pepper
2 tbsp lemon juice
2 tbsp full-fat crème fraiche
8 oz/225 g butter

Put the smoked trout fillets into a food-processor with the parsley and whiz until they are just smooth. Now add the horseradish, the pepper and lemon juice, and pulse to mix them in. Lastly, add the crème fraiche, and pulse until it is incorporated. Divide the mixture between 6 ramekins, smoothing the surface. Put the butter into a small saucepan over a low heat and let it melt as slowly as possible. Do not stir it. Carefully pour the butter, leaving the curd at the bottom of the pan, over each ramekin. Let the butter set, then clingfilm the ramekins and keep them in the fridge.

. . . .

Take the ramekins out of the fridge 20 minutes before you wish to serve them, and discard the clingfilm.

first and light courses

Walnut bread with raisins

*This is not a first course in itself, of course, but it makes such a wonderful –
and, perhaps, surprising – accompaniment to a number of recipes, notably
any that contain smoked fish or a creamy garlic-flavoured dish. As with all
breads, it freezes well, so I've given you a recipe for 3 loaves.*

1½ pints/900 ml hand-hot water
2 tsp sugar
2 tbsp Allinson's dried yeast
1 tbsp salt
2 tbsp honey or Demerara sugar
3 lb/1.35 kg wholewheat *or* strong plain white flour, plus a little extra
4 oz/110 g chopped walnuts, dry-fried
4 oz/110 g best-quality raisins, Lexia if possible

Put ½ pint (300ml) of the water into a bowl, stir in the sugar, then the
yeast and leave it until a head of froth has developed that is at least
double in size to the water beneath it. Mix the remaining water with
the salt and the honey or Demerara sugar.

Now take a large mixing bowl, and stir the frothy yeast liquid with
the honey liquid into the flour. Stir in the walnuts and raisins, and mix
well. Put a couple of handfuls of flour on a work surface, and tip the
sticky dough on to this. Knead, adding more flour if necessary, until
the dough is pliable, and not too sticky, about 2 minutes. Oil 3 x
l-lb/450-g loaf tins, and divide the dough between them. Leave,
covered with a cloth, in a warm place – but not on direct heat – until
the dough has doubled in size. Then carefully (don't thump or bang
them) put them into a preheated hot oven, 420°F/220°C/Gas Mark 7
(top right oven in a 4-door Aga) for 20 minutes. Take out one loaf, tip
it out of its tin and tap its base: it should sound hollow. If it does, take
out the other loaves, and let them cool on a wire rack, but not near
a draught (it toughens the bread). If the loaf does not sound hollow,
put it back and bake for a further 5 minutes.

Never try to fast-thaw bread from the freezer in a microwave oven:
it draws out moisture and the bread will taste stale.

Red onion cream tart

with walnut and Parmesan pastry

It is such a waste not to flavour pastry. I always say this at my demon-strations, and I really cannot say it often enough. In this case the walnuts provide added flavour and a crunchy texture too, while the Parmesan complements the walnuts and the almost caramelized red onions of the filling. You can make and bake the pastry several days in advance, but keep it in an airtight container in the fridge. You can sauté the onions the day before you make the filling, and bake the tart several hours in advance of eating it. Serve it hot, warm or cold – perhaps depending on the weather!

Serves 6

for the pastry
6 oz/175 g flour
4 oz/110 g butter, hard from the fridge, diced
1 tsp icing sugar
2 oz/50 g Parmesan, finely grated
½ tsp salt
3 oz/75 g chopped walnuts

for the filling
3 tbsp olive oil
6 red onions, skinned and thinly sliced
2 cloves garlic, skinned and chopped
1 tsp salt
a good grinding of black pepper
a grating of nutmeg
2 large eggs
2 egg yolks
½ pint/300 ml single cream

To make the pastry, put the flour, butter, icing sugar, Parmesan and salt into a food-processor then whiz until the mixture is the texture of fine crumbs. Then stir in the walnuts by hand. Press this mixture around the sides and base of a 9-in/22-cm flan dish. Put the dish into the fridge for at least 1 hour. Then bake it in a preheated moderate oven, 350°F/180°C/Gas Mark 4 (bottom right oven in a 4-door Aga), for 20 minutes – the pastry should be just coming away from the sides of the tin. Press any slipping pastry back up the sides with the

first and light courses

back of a metal spoon, and bake for a further 5 minutes, if you think it necessary. Take it out and let it cool.

To make the filling, heat the oil in a sauté pan and add the onions. Cook them over a moderate heat, stirring occasionally, for about 10 minutes, then add the garlic and continue to cook for a further 5 minutes or until the onions are much reduced and well softened. Season with salt, pepper and nutmeg, then let the mixture cool. Beat together the eggs, yolks and cream, then stir them into the onions. Pour the filling into the cooled pastry shell. Put the tart carefully into a preheated moderate oven, 350°F/180°C/Gas Mark 4 (bottom right oven in a 4-door Aga), and bake it until the filling is just set in the middle when you gently press it with a finger, about 20–30 minutes.

. . . .

Serve the tart hot, warm or cold, with some vinaigrette-dressed salad leaves.

Blue cheese mousse

with pear and walnut vinaigrette

This is rich – but very good. The pear and walnut vinaigrette counteracts the richness and adds a complementary sweet sharpness to the mousse. Use any blue cheese you like – except Danish Blue, which to me tastes as the nappy bucket used to smell. Melba toast is very good with this, or crisp Italian breadsticks.

Serves 6

4 leaves gelatine *or* 1 sachet powdered gelatine
½ pint/300 ml chicken *or* vegetable stock
1 lb/450 g not-too-harsh blue cheese – for example, Gorgonzola *or* Dunsyre Blue
½ pint/300 ml full-fat crème fraiche
a grating of nutmeg
a good grinding of black pepper
2 egg whites

for the pear and walnut vinaigrette

4 tbsp olive oil
2 tsp balsamic vinegar
1 tbsp lemon juice
pinch of salt
½ tbsp chopped parsley
snipped chives
a good grinding of black pepper
½ tsp caster sugar
4 ripe pears
4 oz/110 g walnuts, chopped and dry-fried

Start by preparing the gelatine: if you are using powdered, sprinkle it with 2 tablespoons cold water and leave it to become spongy. If you are using leaf gelatine, soak the leaves in cold water. Warm the stock, and either dissolve the spongy powdered gelatine in it, gently shaking the saucepan until the granules have dissolved, or lift the soaked leaves from the water and drop them into the stock – they dissolve almost immediately. Leave to cool.

Put the blue cheese and the crème fraiche into a food-processor and pulse until just blended. Then add the cold gelatine mixture, the nutmeg and pepper. Pour this into a bowl and leave it until it starts to set. In a clean bowl, whisk the egg whites until they are stiff. Then, with a large metal spoon, fold them quickly and thoroughly through the blue cheese mixture. Pour it into a serving bowl and leave it to set.

To make the vinaigrette, mix together the olive oil, balsamic vinegar, lemon juice, salt, parsley, chives, pepper and sugar.

. . . .

No more than two to three hours before serving, peel the pears, halve them and remove the cores. Slice them thinly and arrange them on top of the mousse. Scatter over the walnuts and pour over the vinaigrette.

Cucumber mousse

with crab and bacon dressing

This mousse, served in more generous amounts per person, would also make a perfect main course for the summer months. It looks so pretty flecked with green chives, but, every bit as important, its tastes and textures – mousse with crab and crispy bacon – are scrumptious. The affinity between bacon, fish and shellfish of all types never ceases to amaze me!

Serves 6 *You can make the mousse and grill the bacon a day ahead.*

2 cucumbers, peeled (easiest done using a potato peeler)
salt
1 tsp caster sugar
1 tbsp white wine vinegar
2 tbsp snipped chives
4 leaves gelatine *or* 1 sachet powdered gelatine
½ pint/300 ml chicken *or* vegetable stock, warmed
1 pint/600 ml full-fat crème fraiche
2 egg whites
a good grinding of black pepper

for the crab and bacon dressing
3 tbsp mayonnaise (best of all if home-made: see page 250)
½ tsp Tabasco
1 lb/450 g crabmeat, mixed white and brown meat
6 rashers smoked streaky bacon, grilled until crisp then broken into bits

Grate the cucumber and sprinkle it with ½ teaspoon of salt. Leave it for 30 minutes, then drain off the liquid. Mix it with the sugar, vinegar and chives. If you are using powdered gelatine, sprinkle it into 2 tablespoons cold water. If you are using gelatine leaves, soak them in cold water for 10 minutes. Either put the spongy powdered gelatine into the warm stock, and gently shake the pan until the granules have dissolved, or drop the soaked leaves into the warm stock – they will dissolve almost immediately. Leave the stock to cool.

Stir the crème fraiche into the cucumber mixture. Then pour in the cold stock, stir well, and leave it until it is beginning to set. Then, in a clean bowl, whisk the egg whites with a pinch of salt until they are

first and light courses

very stiff. With a large metal spoon fold them quickly and thoroughly through the creamy cucumber mixture, with the pepper. Check the seasoning and stir in a little more salt if necessary. Pour the mixture into a serving bowl – it looks pretty enough as it is, flecked with the chives, and needs no garnish. Cover the bowl with clingfilm, and keep it in the fridge.

To make the dressing, mix the mayonnaise and Tabasco into the crabmeat, then stir in the bacon bits. Do this on the day of serving.

· ·

To serve, put a spoonful of mousse on each plate with a small spoonful of the crab dressing beside it, and a few assorted salad leaves if you like.

Roast aubergine mousse

with tomato, black olive and caper relish

This, for me, is the taste of the Mediterranean. But you must use capers preserved in olive oil. If you can't find any, use the best-quality capers you can buy, drain them of their brine, put them into a jar and immerse them in olive oil for 2 days. Roasting the aubergines imparts a deliciously smoky taste to them. You can make this a day ahead – even two days ahead, though one is better.

Serves 6

4 aubergines, ends cut off
2 tbsp olive oil, plus a little extra to roast the aubergines
4 leaves gelatine *or* 1 sachet powdered gelatine
juice of ½ lemon
½ pint/300 ml chicken *or* vegetable stock, warmed
2 red onions, skinned and chopped
1–2 cloves of garlic, to taste, skinned and chopped
salt
a good grinding of black pepper
½ pint/300 ml full-fat crème fraiche
2 tbsp chopped flat-leaf parsley
2 egg whites

for the tomato, black olive and caper relish

8 large ripe vine tomatoes, skinned, halved, seeded, each half cut into 4
12 black Greek olives, the flesh cut from the stones
3 tsp capers, drained of their oil
1 tbsp olive oil
finely grated zest of 1 lemon
juice of ½ lemon
a good grinding of black pepper (no salt – the olives add enough saltiness)

Preheat the oven to 420°F/220°C/Gas Mark 7.

To make the mousse, start by roasting the aubergines. Lay them on an oiled baking tray, brush them with olive oil and roast them in the hot oven (top right oven in a 4-door Aga) until the skins have darkened and they are soft, about 20–25 minutes. Meanwhile if you are using powdered gelatine, soak it in the lemon juice until it is

first and light courses

spongy, then put it into the warmed stock and shake the pan until all the granules have dissolved. If you are using gelatine leaves, soak them in cold water for 10 minutes then drop them into the stock where they will dissolve almost immediately. Leave to cool.

Heat the olive oil in a sauté pan and sauté the chopped onions for 5 minutes, or until they are soft and transparent. Then add the garlic, and sauté for a further 2 minutes. Season with a teaspoon of salt and plenty of pepper and leave to cool.

Meanwhile, peel the skin from the roast aubergines, put the flesh into a food-processor, then whiz it with the cooled onions and garlic. Whiz in the now cold stock, and scoop the mixture into a bowl. Leave it until it is beginning to set, then stir in the crème fraiche, the lemon juice if you have used loaf gelatine, and the parsley.

In a clean bowl, whisk the egg whites with a pinch of salt until they are stiff. With a large metal spoon, fold them quickly and thoroughly through the aubergine mixture, and pour it into a glass or china serving dish. Cover it, and leave it to set.

. . . .

For the relish, mix together all the ingredients and leave it for several hours to let the flavours mingle. Serve either over the top of the aubergine mousse or hand it separately.

Roast red pepper and aubergine salad

with grilled goat's cheese

The slight sweetness of the caramelized red peppers and aubergines combines delectably with grilled goat's cheese. You can prepare the pepper and aubergine mixture a day in advance, and pop the goat's cheese under the grill for just a minute immediately before serving. Adding the sliced garlic towards the end of the roasting allows it to supply more flavour. If you prefer a gentler contribution from the garlic, roast it from the beginning. In larger quantities, this makes an excellent simple main course salad. (See photograph facing page 65.)

Serves 6

3 medium-sized aubergines, sliced into fat julienne strips
3 red peppers, halved, seeded and sliced into thick strips
4 tbsp olive oil
1 tsp salt
1–2 cloves of garlic, skinned and sliced
a good grinding of black pepper
2 tsp balsamic vinegar
6 x ½-in/1 cm slices goat's cheese log (2–3 oz/50–75 g)

Preheat the oven to 400°F/200°C/Gas Mark 6.

Take a baking tray and line it with baking parchment. Lay on it the peppers and aubergines and mix the olive oil into them with your hands. Sprinkle over the salt, and put it into the hot oven (top right oven in a 4-door Aga) for 20 minutes. Then shuffle the outer pieces of pepper and aubergine towards the centre of the baking tray, and the inner bits to the outer edges. Roast for a further 15–20 minutes. Fork the sliced garlic through the roasting vegetables 5 minutes before you take them out of the oven.

Tip the roasted peppers and aubergines into a bowl, and season well with pepper. Pour in the balsamic vinegar and mix thoroughly. Cover the bowl, and keep it in a cool place.

. . . .

To assemble the salad, divide the roasted vegetables between 6 plates. Line a baking tray with foil, and rub it with a small amount of olive oil. Put the slices of goat's cheese on to the oiled foil, pop it under a red-hot grill and watch the slices like a hawk as you grill on one side only for 45–60 seconds, or until the cheese begins to melt and develop light brown bubbles on the surface. (Do remember that goat's cheese takes so very much less time to melt than does any other type of cheese.) With a palette knife or a fish slice, slip a slice on to each mound of roast peppers and aubergines. Serve immediately.

Warm sautéd chicken liver salad

with fried walnut dressing

When I first ate a warm chicken liver salad, some fifteen years ago, it was served with oyster mushrooms and it was unpleasantly slimy. Ever since then I have put crunch into a chicken liver salad – here with the fried walnuts in the dressing and the crispy bacon bits. This is a most filling dish, so choose a light main course to follow. The livers can be picked over and chopped up several hours in advance, but store them in a bowl that you have first rubbed with olive oil – this prevents a hard line of blood forming on the bowl at the top of the livers, which makes washing-up hell. Make the dressing, prepare the salad leaves and grill the bacon in advance, and then a very few minutes to heat the olive oil and sauté the prepared livers will be all the work needed after your guests have arrived.

Serves 6

for the dressing **3 tbsp olive oil**
4 oz/110 g walnuts, chopped
½ tsp salt
1 tsp balsamic vinegar

3 rashers smoked streaky bacon, grilled till crisp, the fat saved
1–2 tbsp olive oil
1¼ lb/675 g fresh (not frozen) chicken livers – stringy or green bits discarded – chopped
pinch of salt
a good grinding of black pepper

assorted salad leaves

First make the dressing: heat the olive oil in a sauté or frying pan, then put in the walnuts and the salt. Stir from time to time over a moderate heat, until the walnuts are almost crisp, then add the balsamic vinegar. Pour it into a small bowl and set it aside.

. . . .

Break up the bacon into tiny bits. When you are ready to cook the livers – which takes only a couple of minutes – heat the olive oil in a sauté pan, and add the bacon fat. Then put in the livers, and stir them around until they are brown on the outside, but still pale pink in the middle. Season with salt and freshly ground pepper, stir well, then add the bacon and take the pan off the heat.

Divide the salad leaves between 6 plates, and spoon the livers and bacon over them. Pour a spoonful of the walnut dressing over each heap of livers and serve warm.

Chicken liver and pistachio terrine

with Madeira, raisin and shallot relish

The relish can be made several days in advance, and kept, covered, in the fridge. Just a small spoonful per person sets off the chicken liver and pistachio terrine to perfection. The terrine improves for being made a day in advance.

Serves 6

4 oz/110 g butter
2 small onions, skinned and chopped
1 clove garlic, skinned and chopped
1½ lb/675 g fresh chicken livers, stringy or green bits discarded to leave you with 1 lb/450 g
3 tbsp brandy
¼ pint/150 ml double cream
salt
a good grinding of black pepper
4 oz/110 g shelled pistachios

for the relish
1 oz/25 g butter
1 tbsp olive oil
3 banana shallots, very thinly sliced
¼ pint/150 ml Madeira
4 oz/110 g best-quality plump and juicy raisins, such as Lexia

To make the terrine melt the butter in a sauté pan and sauté the chopped onions until they are soft and transparent. Then add the garlic and the chicken livers. Stir everything around until the livers are brown but still pink inside. Add the brandy, let it bubble, then pour in the cream and stir. Season with salt and pepper, then let it cool. When it is cold whiz it in a food-processor until it is smooth.

Line a 2-lb/900-g terrine or loaf tin with clingfilm. Wrap the pistachios in kitchen paper and bash them with a rolling-pin to break them up. Mix them into the chicken-liver mixture in the food-processor bowl (don't whiz them: do this by hand) then scrape it all into the mould. Bang it a couple of times on the work surface to remove any air pockets, cover the top and put it into the fridge overnight.

first and light courses

To make the relish, heat the butter and oil together in a saucepan, then put in the shallots. Cook them over a moderate heat until they are very soft. Don't let them colour. Then add the Madeira and the raisins, and simmer gently until the Madeira has virtually evaporated. Put the contents of the pan into a small bowl, and store it in a cool place.

. . . .

To serve, tip the terrine out of the tin on to a plate and slice it. Put a slice on each plate with a dollop of the relish beside it.

Chicken and avocado terrine

This dish has distinct and delicate tastes, all complementary. The chives, lemon juice and mayonnaise are all wonderful with chicken and avocado, and the texture is fairly smooth. Perfect for summer eating. The terrine can be made a day in advance, providing that it is kept, covered, in the fridge. Let it come to room temperature 20 minutes or so before you serve it, to get rid of 'fridge chill', which numbs flavour and rubberizes texture.

Serves 6

4 x 4 oz/110 g chicken breasts, preferably organic
1½ pints/900 ml chicken stock
4 leaves gelatine *or* 1 sachet powdered gelatine
about 2 tsp Tabasco
½ pint/300 ml mayonnaise, preferably home-made
2 tbsp snipped chives
2 large (or 3 small) avocados
3 tbsp lemon juice
salt
freshly ground black pepper
2 egg whites

Preheat the oven to 350°F/180°C/Gas Mark 4.

Put the chicken breasts in an ovenproof dish with the stock, cover with baking parchment and bake in the moderate oven (bottom right oven in a 4-door Aga) for 25–30 minutes, or until the juices run clear when you stick the point of a knife into the thickest part.

Meanwhile, soak the leaf gelatine in cold water for 10 minutes or the powdered gelatine in 2 tablespoons of cold water and leave it to become spongy.

Strain off ½ pint/300 ml of the chicken stock and, if you are using powdered gelatine, stir it into the stock until the granules have dissolved. If you are using leaf gelatine, lift it out of the water, drop it into the hot stock and stir briefly – it melts almost instantly. Stir in the Tabasco and leave to cool.

Remove the skin from the chicken breasts, cut the flesh into chunks and put it into the food-processor with the stock. Pulse the chicken until it is coarsely smooth, not pulverized. Pour the contents of the food-processor into a bowl, and leave in a cool place until it is beginning to set. Then fold into it the mayonnaise and snipped chives. Cut each avocado in half, flick away the stones, and remove the skin. Dice the flesh as neatly as you can, about thumbnail-size. Put it into a bowl, and toss it with the lemon juice.

Taste the chicken mixture and season it with salt and pepper. Whisk the egg whites with a pinch of salt until they are stiff. With a large metal spoon, fold them thoroughly through the chicken mixture, with the diced avocado.

Line a 2½ lb/1.2 kg loaf or terrine tin with clingfilm. Spoon and scrape the chicken and avocado mixture into the lined terrine tin or dish. Bang it gently on the work surface a couple of times to get rid of any air pockets, cover the top, and put it into the fridge to set.

· ·

To serve, tip the terrine out on to a serving plate, carefully peel off the clingfilm, and slice. Serve it with assorted vinaigrette-dressed salad leaves.

Cream cheese, garlic and chilli terrine

with avocado salsa

This creamy-textured terrine can be made a day in advance, but it is vital to cover the terrine dish with clingfilm to prevent the garlic from leaching into other foods in the fridge. The salsa gives a deliciously sharp complementary flavour and a contrasting texture. It, too, can be made a day in advance. This dish is perfect for a summer lunch, accompanied by a mixed leaf salad, and some warm bread or rolls.

The salsa is spiked with coriander, to which I am becoming addicted, but if you don't feel the same way about it, substitute parsley, or perhaps chervil. The lime juice helps to prevent the avocado flesh discolouring if you make the salsa a day in advance.

Serves 6

4 leaves gelatine, *or* 1 sachet powdered gelatine

½ pint/300 ml chicken or vegetable stock

1–2 fat cloves of garlic, skinned

½ tsp salt

1¼ lb/675 g cream cheese, such as Philadelphia

juice of 1 lemon

½ tsp dried chilli flakes

2 tbsp chopped flat-leaf parsley (about 2 handfuls before chopping)

2 tbsp snipped chives (a small bunch)

a good grinding of black pepper

for the avocado salsa

3 ripe avocados

zest and juice of 1 lime

6 tomatoes, skinned, halved, seeded and finely diced

about ¼ skinned red onion, finely diced

2 sticks celery, washed, trimmed and finely sliced

2 tbsp roughly chopped coriander leaves

½ tsp salt

 a good grinding of black pepper

2 tbsp olive oil

1 tsp balsamic vinegar

first and light courses

If you are using leaf gelatine, put it to soak in cold water for 10 minutes. Then warm the stock, and drop in the soaked leaves, which will dissolve almost immediately. If you are using powdered gelatine, sprinkle it into the stock in a small saucepan. Let it become spongy, then over a *very* gentle heat shake the pan until the granules have dissolved. Do not let the liquid boil. Leave it to cool.

Crush the garlic with the salt. Put the cream cheese into a food-processor and whiz, then add the garlic, the gelatine mixture, the lemon juice, chilli, parsley, chives and pepper. Meanwhile, line a Pyrex or metal terrine with clingfilm. Pour in the cheese mixture and bang the terrine a couple of times on a work surface to get rid of any air pockets. Then cover the surface with clingfilm and put it into the fridge to set. Allow at least 4 hours, or, better, overnight. To turn it out – it couldn't be simpler – take off the covering clingfilm, turn it face down on a pretty serving plate, and lift off the clingfilm.

To make the salsa, cut each avocado in half. Cut the skin in three sections on each half, then peel it off. Flick out the stones, and carefully dice the avocado flesh into a bowl. Stir in the lime zest and juice. Then add all the other ingredients of the salsa and mix well together – gently, so that the avocado doesn't turn into a mush. Closely cover the surface of the salsa with clingfilm – to prevent discolouring – and put the bowl into the fridge.

. . . .

To serve, slice the terrine thickly and put a dollop of salsa either beside it on the plates or half over it.

Deep-fried Parmesan rice balls

with tomato and chilli sauce

These are awfully good, if rather messy to make. Have a box of thin plastic gloves to hand for such tasks! You can make the risotto and the Parmesan balls a day in advance, but keep them covered and cold before you deep-fry them. The velvety chilli sauce is a striking contrast to the crunchy rice balls.

Serves 6

4 tbsp olive oil

2 onions, skinned and very finely chopped

1–2 cloves of garlic, skinned and finely chopped

6 oz/175 g risotto rice, such as Arborio *or* Carnaroli

1½ pints/900 ml chicken stock

2 large egg yolks

3 oz/75 g Parmesan, coarsely grated

salt

a good grinding of black pepper

2 tbsp chopped flat-leaf parsley

6–8 oz/175–225 g white or brown breadcrumbs (made from day-old baked – not steamed – bread)

oil for frying

for the sauce

3 tbsp olive oil

2 onions, skinned and chopped

1 clove of garlic, skinned and chopped

2 sticks celery, washed and trimmed

2 x 15 oz/400 g cans chopped tomatoes

½ tsp salt

a good grinding of black pepper

½ tsp sugar

½ tsp dried chilli flakes

Heat the olive oil in a sauté pan and put in the onions, then cook until they are soft and transparent. Add the chopped garlic and the rice. Stir the rice around for 2–3 minutes, so that each grain is coated with oil. Then stir in a small amount of chicken stock over a moderate heat. Add more stock as it evaporates, stirring from time to time, until it is all incorporated. Take the pan off the heat, then beat in the egg yolks, and the Parmesan. Season with salt and pepper and leave to cool. When it is cold, stir in the parsley.

Line a baking tray with baking parchment. If you have them, put on a pair of thin plastic gloves; otherwise dip your hands into cold water. Roll the rice mixture into balls about the size of a large golf ball; make them as even as possible. Coat each one with breadcrumbs, and put them on the baking tray, then cover and store the rice balls in the fridge. Return to room temperature for 30 minutes before frying.

To deep-fry – you don't need a deep-fryer – take a large saucepan and pour in the oil to a depth of about 4 in/10 cm. Have ready a few cubes of bread to test the heat of the oil – they will sizzle when it's ready. Remove them before you cook the rice balls, 3–4 at a time, until they are golden brown. Scoop them from the oil with a slotted spoon and put them on a large, warm serving dish, lined with several thicknesses of absorbent kitchen paper. They will keep warm satisfactorily in a low oven .

To make the sauce, heat the oil in a saucepan and add the onions, garlic and celery. Cook over a moderate heat until the onion is soft and transparent, then add the tomatoes, the salt, pepper, sugar and chilli. Stir well, then simmer for 10–15 minutes. Let the mixture cool, then liquidize it and pour the velvety smooth sauce into a clean saucepan to reheat as required.

. . . .

Serve 2, 3 or 4 rice balls per person, depending on appetite, with the tomato and chilli sauce handed separately.

Frittata with sautéd leeks and Brie

This is a terrifically versatile dish – another first-course recipe that makes an excellent light lunch. It is also perfect picnic food, because it won't melt or slop in transit. And you have to make it several hours before you plan to eat it. It is essential to cook it very slowly so that the eggs are just set around the filling. You can cook the leeks a day before you make the frittata, if you like, and you can slice the Brie ahead too. I don't bother to remove the top and bottom rind, just the edge.

Serves 6

4 tbsp olive oil
6 medium-sized leeks, trimmed, washed and thinly sliced
a grating of nutmeg
1 tsp salt
a good grinding of black pepper
10 large eggs
1 tsp Tabasco
8 oz/225 g Brie, sliced into 6, edge rind removed

Heat 3 tablespoons of the oil in a sauté pan and cook the sliced leeks until they are very soft. Stir in the nutmeg, salt and pepper.

Beat the eggs with the Tabasco. Heat the remaining oil in a 7-in/18-cm crêpe or frying pan and pour in the egg mixture – it should pretty well fill the pan to the brim. Carefully fork in the leeks. Lower the heat under the pan and let the eggs set: the mixture should not rise up the sides of the pan but if this happens reduce the heat. When the base is firmly set, preheat the grill to medium, and arrange the 6 slices of Brie, pointed ends towards the centre, on top of the frittata. Put the pan under the grill and leave it just until the eggs have firmed up on the top.

. . . .

Then slip the frittata on to a serving plate and cut into wedges. Scatter some assorted salad leaves around it.

first and light courses

Frittata with roasted cherry tomatoes,

black olives and feta cheese

Here is another version of a frittata, one that contrasts well with the Frittata with Sautéd Leeks and Brie on the facing page if you like to offer a choice. There is no need for salt: the feta cheese adds quite enough saltiness, even for me! Slow-roasting the halved cherry tomatoes slightly caramelizes them. Alternatively, use 6 chopped sun-dried tomatoes, if you prefer them. **Serves 6**

1 lb/450 g cherry tomatoes, halved
4 tbsp olive oil
8 juicy black olives, flesh cut off from stones
10 large eggs
a good grinding of black pepper
6 oz/175 g feta cheese, cut into fairly small dice, about thumbnail-size

Start by roasting the tomatoes – this can be done a day in advance. Lay a sheet of baking parchment on a roasting tray. Put the prepared tomatoes on it and, using your hands, rub two tablespoons of the olive oil into them. Roast in a fairly slow oven, 250°F/125°C/Gas Mark ½ (top left oven in a 4-door Aga), for 1½ hours. Mix with the black olives in a bowl and set aside somewhere cool.

To make the frittata, beat the eggs with the black pepper. Heat the remaining oil in a 7-in/18-cm crêpe or frying pan and pour in the egg mixture – it should pretty well fill the pan to the brim. Over a slow heat let the eggs just set: the mixture should not rise up the sides of the pan but if this happens reduce the heat. Carefully fork in the diced feta and the tomato and olive mixture, and preheat the grill to medium. When the base of the frittata is firmly set, put the pan under the preheated grill. Cook until the surface where the egg shows through is just firm.

. . . .

Slip the frittata on to a serving plate and cut into wedges. Serve hot, or barely warm.

Cold fresh tomato and basil soup

Serves 6   *This is easy, and can be made a day ahead.*

12 ripe tomatoes, from the vine, skinned, halved and seeded
½ red onion, skinned and chopped
1 pint/600 ml chicken *or* vegetable stock
1 tsp salt
a good grinding of black pepper
½ tsp caster sugar
2 tbsp basil leaves
¼ pint/150 ml double cream

Put the tomatoes into a blender with the onion, stock, salt, pepper and sugar and whiz until smooth. Add the basil leaves, and whiz briefly, then whiz in the cream. Pour the contents of the blender into a bowl, cover and keep it in the fridge until you are ready to serve it, with Parmesan Crisps (see opposite) or bread.

first and light courses

Parmesan crisps

These make a lovely accompaniment to soup and especially the fresh, summer-tasting Tomato and Basil Soup opposite. They are also ideal as a simple savoury at the end of dinner, or with drinks beforehand. Allow 3 per person.

Serves 6

6 oz/175 g Parmesan, grated

Preheat the oven to 420°F/220°C/Gas Mark 7.

Line a baking tray with baking parchment. Take a plain 2½-in/7-cm scone-cutter, pour in a tablespoon of Parmesan, and with the back of a teaspoon, press it down to a depth of ⅛ in/½ cm. Lift off the scone-cutter carefully – some of the Parmesan may fall off the sides of the disc but don't worry – it's almost impossible to avoid this. Repeat until the Parmesan is all used up. Space the discs quite far apart on the baking sheet. You will need to bake them in 2–3 batches, depending on the size of your baking tray. Bake them in the hot oven (top right oven in a 4-door Aga) for 7 minutes, then take them out of the oven – they should be bubbling and dark golden brown. Wait till bubbling stops, then, if they are very misshapen and you mind, even them up with the scone-cutter. I never bother, unless they have run together.

. . . .

Serve the Parmesan crisps on the day you make them.

Avocado and lime soup

A light, refreshing soup, ideal for late spring, summer and early autumn evenings. It takes only a few minutes to prepare. It can be made in the morning to eat that evening. (See photograph facing page 64.)

3 tbsp olive oil
2 onions, skinned and chopped
1 fat clove of garlic, skinned and chopped
1 pint/600 ml chicken *or* vegetable stock
4 fairly large avocados, 5 if they are smaller
3 limes
½ tsp salt
a good grinding of pepper
½ pint/300 ml single cream

Heat the oil in a frying pan and cook the onions until they are soft and turning golden brown at the edges. Then add the garlic and cook for another minute. Pour in the stock and bring it to a simmer, leave it for a minute, then take the pan off the heat and let it cool.

Halve the avocados, flick out the stones, then scoop the flesh into the blender. Pour in the stock mixture, add the zest of 1 lime and the juice of 2, then whiz. Pour the thick soup into a bowl and season with salt and pepper. Stir in the cream. If the soup seems too thick, add a little more stock, or cream, until the consistency is as you like it.

. . . .

Serve the soup cold, but not chilled, in soup plates, with a thin slice of the remaining lime floating on top.

Roast red pepper and celery soup

This rather unlikely combination, of red peppers and celery, was the result of an experiment one evening for our guests here at Kinloch. The result was such a success that two or three people asked for the recipe. It is a perfect first-course soup because it's thin but intensely flavoured. **Serves 6**

6 red peppers, halved and seeded
3 tbsp olive oil, plus a little extra
1 onion, skinned and chopped
1 head celery, washed, trimmed and chopped
1½ pints/900 ml chicken stock
½–1 tsp salt
a good grinding of black pepper
1 tsp balsamic vinegar
6 tsp crème fraiche, to garnish

Preheat the oven to 400°F/200°C/Gas Mark 6.

Cut each pepper in half, scoop out the seeds, and put the pepper halves, skin side up, on a baking tray lined with baking parchment. Rub them with olive oil, and roast for 20–25 minutes in the hot oven (top right oven in a 4-door Aga). By then the peppers should be changing colour. Take the tray out of the oven.

Meanwhile, heat the olive oil in a saucepan, put in the onion and cook for 3–5 minutes until it is soft. Then add the celery, stir it into the onion, and cook for 2 minutes. Pour in the stock, and when the liquid starts to simmer, add the peppers. Half cover the pan with its lid, and simmer gently for 15 minutes, or until the celery is tender. Take the pan off the heat, let it cool a little, then liquidize until it is smooth. Sieve the soup and put it back into the rinsed saucepan. Season with salt, pepper and balsamic vinegar.

. . . .

To serve, reheat the soup, pour it into soup plates and drop a dollop of crème fraiche into the middle of each helping.

Parsnip, lime and ginger soup

Parsnips are a sweet vegetable so the lime gives this warming soup a welcome sharpness. Ginger goes well with all root vegetables, so don't be afraid to use the entire amount suggested in the recipe: the longer ginger cooks the milder it becomes. The result is a warm-tasting, thick, velvety soup.

Serves 6

3 tbsp olive oil
2 onions, skinned and chopped
4 average-sized parsnips, peeled, trimmed and cut into chunks
2-in/5-cm piece fresh root ginger, skinned and chopped
1 fat clove of garlic, skinned and chopped
1½ pints/900 ml chicken stock
3 limes
½ tsp salt
a good grinding of black pepper
2 tbsp finely chopped flat-leaf parsley

Heat the oil in a saucepan, put in the onions and cook until they are soft and transparent. Then add the prepared parsnips with the ginger. Continue to cook, stirring occasionally, for 7–10 minutes. Then stir in the garlic and the stock. Bring it to a simmer, half cover the pan with its lid and cook gently until the largest chunks of parsnip are soft. Take the pan off the heat and add the zest of 2 limes, salt and pepper. Let the soup cool a little, then whiz in a blender until it is smooth. Add the juice of 2 limes, taste and correct the seasoning if necessary.

. . . .

To serve, reheat the soup and stir in the parsley just before you ladle it into soup plates. Float a slice of lime on top of each helping.

first and light courses

Ham and butterbean vegetable soup

This soup is close to a stew, and is most sustaining and satisfying on dark, cold winter days. I would follow it with a steamed syrup and ginger pudding, with vanilla cream custard. And, given the chance, I'd eat it twice a week throughout winter! You can make this 2 days in advance.

Serves 6

4 tbsp olive oil
2 onions, skinned and finely chopped
2 leeks, trimmed, washed and thinly sliced
2 cloves of garlic, skinned and chopped
3 carrots, peeled and diced thumbnail-size
3 parsnips, peeled and diced thumbnail-size
2 sticks celery, trimmed, washed and sliced
½ head celeriac, peeled and diced thumbnail-size
8 oz/225 g butter beans, soaked overnight in a large bowl of water
2 pints/1.2 litres good ham stock
plenty of ground black pepper
a grating of nutmeg
salt

Heat the oil in a large flameproof casserole or saucepan and sauté the onions and leeks until the onions are transparent. Stir in the garlic, cook for a minute then add the rest of the prepared vegetables and the butter beans. Pour in the stock, and stir occasionally until the liquid is simmering. Cover the pan with its lid, and cook gently for half an hour. If you have an Aga, put the simmering soup, lid on, in the coolest oven for 2 hours.

Taste the soup, and season with pepper, nutmeg, and salt if it is needed. Keep the soup in a cool place until you need to reheat it.

. . . .

To serve, reheat the soup and ladle it into bowls.

Potato soup with crispy bacon bits

Serves 6

This is a simple soup, but very tasty. It's adaptable, too: make it as a first course, or serve it as a more sustaining lunchtime snack – liquidize half of the soup then stir it into the rest, with its chunks of potato and slices of onion.

3 tbsp olive oil

3 onions, skinned and thinly sliced

4 medium-sized potatoes, peeled and cut into ½-in/1 cm chunks

1–2 cloves of garlic, to taste, skinned and chopped

1½ pints/900 ml chicken stock

½–1 tsp salt

a good grinding of black pepper

a grating of nutmeg

2 tbsp chopped flat-leaf parsley

12 rashers smoked streaky bacon, grilled until crisp then broken into bits

Heat the oil in a saucepan, put in the onions and cook, stirring from time to time, for 5–7 minutes or until they are turning golden brown at the edges. Then add the potatoes and garlic and stir well. Continue to cook over a low heat for a couple of minutes, then pour in the stock. Bring it to a simmer, half cover the pan with its lid and cook for 10 minutes or until the largest piece of potato is soft when squished against the side of the pan, then season with salt, pepper and nutmeg. Take the pan off the heat and let the soup cool a little, then liquidize until it is very smooth. Keep it in a cool place.

. . . .

To serve, reheat the soup and stir in the parsley with the bacon bits just before you ladle it into the soup plates. Don't leave the bacon in the hot soup for too long or it will become flabby.

first and light courses

Creamy Brussels sprout and chestnut soup

I love Brussels sprouts, and this is one of my favourite soups. It will only be as good as the sprouts, though, so don't make the mistake of thinking that this is a good way to use up ageing yellow ones. They must be fresh, green and hard. None the less, you can make the soup a day ahead without any loss of quality and flavour.

Serves 6

3 tbsp olive oil
2 onions, skinned and chopped
4 oz/110 g chestnuts, tinned or sous vide
1 lb/450 g Brussels sprouts, trimmed and halved
1½ pints/900 ml chicken stock
½–1 tsp salt
a good grinding of black pepper
a grating of nutmeg
6 tsp crème fraiche to garnish
6 rashers smoked *or* unsmoked streaky bacon, grilled till crisp then broken up

Heat the olive oil in a saucepan, put in the onions and cook until they are soft and transparent. Add the chestnuts and sprouts, and cook with the onions for 4–5 minutes. Stir in the stock, bring it to a simmer, then half cover the pan with its lid and cook gently until the sprouts are soft but not overcooked – about 10 minutes. Take the pan off the heat, let the soup cool a little then liquidize until it is smooth. Pour it back into the saucepan, taste, and season with salt pepper and nutmeg.

. . . .

To serve, reheat the soup and ladle it into the soup plates. Put a dollop of crème fraiche and a few crisp bacon bits into each helping.

Fish and sea

food

We are told by the Health Police that we should eat fish, especially oily varieties, at least three times a week and this chapter contains recipes for dishes you can serve as a first or as a main course. Some are almost embarrassingly simple, such as Squid and Scallops with Olive Oil, Lemon and Parsley on page 96, but then, the better the ingredient the less you need to do with it.

Fish is fast food, true convenience cooking, and it is ruined by overcooking – no amount of rich, delicious sauce will mask the taste and texture of dried-out fish. You can prepare fish well in advance of cooking it – have a look at the recipe for Baked Cod (or Hake) with Spiced Green Lentils and Coriander Pesto (page 70).

In this chapter I am particularly proud of the recipes for Quenelles on page 65, which I had thought far above my capabilities and too lengthy in preparation. Henrietta Thewes inspired me to make them – and the two versions I give here are easier to make than you could imagine and convenient too.

Fish is good eaten cold, too, and not just shellfish: try the mouth-watering Halibut in a Herb Dressing on page 64 for a summer lunch or dinner.

Char-grilled monkfish, marinated in lime juice

with chilli, red onion and coriander with coriander and lime crème fraiche dressing

A long title for a dish we put together as a first course for dinner for fifty of us on the night before our second daughter Isabella's wedding in November 2000. It was a great success and for me will always be associated with that weekend. It has to be made several hours in advance, and the simple accompanying dressing can be made the previous day. We mixed crabmeat and langostinos – our local sweet, succulent squat lobsters – with the marinating monkfish. You can use other shellfish, too, or not, as you choose. If you can't be bothered to get out the barbecue, buy a disposable one to char-grill the monkfish fillets – it really is worthwhile for the flavour. The quantities given are for a main course. (See photograph facing page 96.)

Serves 6

for the dressing
½ pint/300 ml full-fat crème fraiche
finely grated zest of 1 lime
1 tbsp chopped coriander
salt and a good grinding of black pepper

3 tbsp olive oil
finely grated zest of 2 limes, and their juice
½ red onion, skinned and very finely diced
1 birdseye chilli, slit open, seeded and finely sliced
½ tsp salt
½ tsp caster sugar
a good grinding of black pepper
2 tbsp chopped coriander
1½ lb/675 g monkfish fillets, trimmed of all membrane
8 oz/225 g cooked langostinos *or* prawn tails, *or* 8 oz/225 g crabmeat,
  ***or* a mixture of both**

To make the dressing, mix together the crème fraiche (and it *must* be full-fat: so much creamier and more delicious), lime zest, chopped coriander and seasonings. Cover and keep in the fridge.

Make the monkfish marinade: mix together the olive oil, lime zest and juice, onion, chilli, salt, sugar, pepper and coriander. Brush each monkfish fillet with olive oil and char-grill them, turning them over so

fish and seafood

that they cook evenly. Depending on their size they will take anything from 1–3 minutes. Take them off the grill and cut them into 1 inch/2.5 cm chunks, put them into a bowl and pour over the marinade. Stir well. Leave it to cool, then stir in the crabmeat, langostinos, or both. Leave for 4–6 hours or overnight.

. . . .

Serve with a mixed leaf salad, and hand the dressing separately.

Spiced monkfish

with almonds, lemon and ginger

Serves 6

The spices and nuts in this dish make it a most intensely flavoured and yummy main course. I serve it with boiled rice, and a mixed leaf salad. The monkfish can be cut up and left, covered in the fridge, several hours ahead.

2-in/5-cm piece root ginger, skinned and chopped

2 cloves of garlic, skinned and finely chopped

1 tsp turmeric

3 oz/75 g flaked *or* whole almonds

1 tsp cornflour

4 tbsp light olive oil

4 banana shallots, skinned and thinly sliced

2 red peppers, halved, seeded and thinly sliced

1–2 birdseye chillies, slit open, seeded and sliced

finely grated zest of 1 lemon

2 tsp sesame oil

2 lb/900 g monkfish, membranes discarded, cut into 1-in/2.5-cm chunks

1 14-oz/400-g can coconut milk

2 tbsp chopped coriander

½ tsp salt

a good grinding of black pepper

Put the ginger, garlic, turmeric, almonds and cornflour into a food processor and whiz to a paste.

Heat the olive oil in a sauté pan and cook the shallots, peppers and chillies over a moderate heat for 4–5 minutes, or until the shallots are soft. Stir in the ginger paste, the lemon zest and the sesame oil and cook for a further minute. Raise the heat, add the chunks of monkfish and stir them around until they are opaque. Pour in the coconut milk, stirring till it bubbles gently, then add the chopped coriander and season with salt and pepper.

. . . .

Keep the contents of the pan warm, without continuing to cook, by placing in a very low oven until you are ready to serve.

fish and seafood

Aromatic stir-fried monkfish

This is a magical dish. I have used monkfish here but you could substitute large prawns, if you prefer. The dish can be prepared in advance, and takes minutes to cook. Serve with steamed sugarsnap peas and boiled basmati rice – which, incidentally, keeps warm for up to an hour and a half in a covered dish in a low oven.

Serves 6

2 lb/900 g monkfish, membrane discarded, cut into 1 inch/2.5 cm chunks
12 spring onions, trimmed and sliced diagonally into 1-inch/2.5-cm strips
2-in/5-cm piece ginger, skinned and finely chopped
4 cloves of garlic, skinned and finely chopped
½ stick lemon grass, finely chopped
1 rounded tsp cornflour
3 tsp sesame oil
3 tbsp strong (dark) soy sauce
3 tbsp medium sherry
3 tbsp olive oil
2 red peppers, halved, seeded and thinly sliced
½ pint/300 ml chicken stock

Put the prepared fish into a bowl, covered, in the fridge until you are ready to cook it. Stir together the spring onions, ginger, garlic, and lemon grass in a bowl, and cover them closely with clingfilm. Mix together the cornflour, sesame oil, soy sauce and sherry.

. . . .

When you are ready to cook, heat the olive oil in a large sauté pan, and put in the red peppers. Cook them over a high heat, stirring, until they soften. Add the spring onions and stir-fry for a couple of minutes. Then pour in the sesame oil mixture, and stir well as the mixture thickens and bubbles. Add the stock and stir until it is simmering. Lastly, drop in the monkfish and stir it around until it turns opaque, 2½–3 minutes. Serve immediately.

Halibut in a herb dressing

This is a cold dish, eminently suitable for a special occasion in warm weather. It is a simple, delicious recipe, convenient, too: it has to be made several hours ahead in order to let the fish cool. The dressing can be made two days in advance. Serve the fish surrounded by salad leaves, herbs and petals.

Serves 6

1½ lb/675 g halibut, filleted and skinned
3 tbsp olive oil
1 lemon, thinly sliced

for the dressing
5 tbsp olive oil
3 tsp balsamic vinegar
½ tsp caster sugar
½ tsp salt
a good grinding of black pepper
3 tbsp chopped flat-leaf parsley, snipped chives and dill

leaves, herbs and petals, to serve

Preheat the oven to 350°F/180°C/Gas Mark 4.

Line a baking tray with a sheet of baking parchment. Lay on it the fish, cover it with the olive oil and then the sliced lemon. Put another sheet of baking parchment over the top and bake in the moderate oven (bottom right oven in a 4-door Aga) for about 15 minutes. Meanwhile, mix together the ingredients for the dressing, if you haven't already made it.

As soon as the fish is cooked, take it out of the oven, remove the lemon slices, and spoon the dressing over the hot fish, which will absorb the flavours as it cools. When it has cooled, spoon the fish, broken up, with the dressing, on to a serving plate. Keep it in a cool place until you are ready to serve it.

. . . .

Surround the fish with the leaves, herbs and petals, and serve.

Avocado and lime soup (page 50)

fish and seafood

Quenelles

Traditionally, quenelles are made with pike, which I find an uninteresting fish, but Henrietta Thewes showed me that they are just as successful made with other fish, that they are not difficult to make, and that they are both delicious and convenient. Here are two recipes for them, one with salmon, the other with smoked and fresh haddock. You can make the quenelle mixture and the sauces up to a day in advance. The quenelles take 5 minutes to poach – a couple of minutes longer if you do a large panful of them – and keep warm in their sauce, in a low oven, most obligingly for 30–45 minutes. The Chive Cream Sauce below goes just as well with the salmon quenelles.

Serves 6

Smoked and fresh haddock quenelles with chive cream sauce

1 lb/450 g smoked haddock, filleted
8 oz/225 g fresh haddock, filleted
1 large egg
2 egg whites
½ pint/300 ml double cream
½ oz or so/15 g parsley
a good grinding of black pepper
a grating of nutmeg
4–5 pints/2.4–3 litres stock

½ pint/300 ml double cream   *for the chive*
1 tbsp lemon juice   *cream sauce*
2 tbsp snipped chives

Put the fish into a food-processor with the egg, egg whites, cream, parsley, pepper and nutmeg. Whiz until smooth and green-flecked. Scrape the mixture into a bowl, cover it, and put it into the fridge for 3–4 hours or overnight.

To make the cream sauce, put the cream, lemon juice and chives into a saucepan, bring it to a simmer, and, stirring, cook for 2 minutes. Cool and store in the fridge.

Roast red pepper and aubergine salad with grilled goat's cheese (page 34)

About an hour before your guests arrive, pour enough stock into a sauté pan to fill it 2 1/2–3 inches/6–7.5 cm deep, and bring it to the boil. Meanwhile grease a large ovenproof dish. When the stock is boiling fast, form neat, even egg shapes of the fish mixture with 2 tablespoons, and slip them into the stock. You should have enough for 12. Poach the quenelles for 5 minutes, turning them over once. When they are ready, put them into the greased dish. Reheat the sauce and pour it over the quenelles – it just coats their surface. Cover the dish, and keep it warm in a low oven until you are ready to serve.

Salmon quenelles with creamy tomato sauce

1½ lb/675 g salmon, preferably organic, filleted
2 anchovy fillets, drained
1 large egg
2 egg whites
½ pint/300 ml double cream
½–1 tsp Tabasco
a good grinding of black pepper
a grating of nutmeg
4–5 pints/2.4–3 litres stock

for the creamy tomato sauce

2 oz/50 g butter
1 red onion, skinned and finely chopped
4 ripe, vine tomatoes, skinned, seeded and chopped
juice of 1 lemon
½ pint double cream (300ml)
½ tsp salt and a good grinding of black pepper

fish and seafood

Put the salmon and anchovies into a food-processor with the egg, egg whites, cream, Tabasco, pepper and nutmeg, then whiz until smooth. Scrape the mixture into a bowl, cover it, and put it into the fridge for 3–4 hours or overnight.

To make the sauce, melt the butter in a saucepan and cook the onion until it is very soft. Add the tomatoes, lemon juice and cream, and simmer for 2 minutes, stirring. Take the pan off the heat, whiz the contents in a blender or food-processor and season. Set aside.

. . . .

About an hour before your guests arrive, pour enough stock into a large saucepan to fill it 2½–3 in/6–7.5 cm deep, and bring it to the boil. Grease an ovenproof dish. When the stock is boiling fast, form the fish mixture into neat, even egg shapes with 2 tablespoons and slip them (you will have about 12) into the stock. Poach them for 5 minutes, turning them over once during that time. When they are done lift them with a slotted spoon and put them into the buttered dish.

Reheat the sauce, pour it over the fish, cover the dish and keep it warm in a low oven until you are ready to serve.

Baked halibut

with creamy watercress and lime sauce

Halibut is my favourite fish for special occasions, but this sauce goes beautifully with other firm-fleshed white fish, such as cod or hake. The time it takes to steam-bake whichever fish you use depends on the thickness of the fillets. Judge it for yourself by carefully investigating the thickest bit of fish with 2 forks. If it looks a bit rare (raw!) for you, cover it again and cook it for a further 5 minutes.

Serves 6

6 x 6 oz/175 g fillets halibut
3 oz/75 g butter, cut into 6
juice of 1 lime

for the sauce
2 oz/50 g butter
1 onion, *or* 2 shallots, skinned and diced
½ pint/300 ml chicken or fish stock
½ pint/300 ml double cream
finely grated zest and juice of 1 lime (wash the lime first)
½ tsp salt
a good grinding of black pepper
2 oz/50 g watercress, steamed till just wilted

First prepare the fish. Cover a baking tray with baking parchment., then lay on it the fish. Feel for and remove any remaining bones. Put a piece of butter on each fillet, and a few drops of lime juice. Cover with a second sheet of baking parchment. Keep the fish in a cool place until you are ready to bake it.

Make the sauce: melt the butter in a saucepan, put in the onion or shallots and cook for 2–3 minutes. Pour in the stock and simmer gently until it has virtually evaporated. Add the cream, and bring it to the boil, then cook, stirring, until it thickens: about 2 minutes' fast boiling. Take the pan off the heat, add the lime juice and zest, salt and pepper. Then pour the sauce into a food-processor with the watercress and whiz until it is smooth. Transfer to a bowl, cover and keep in the fridge.

fish and seafood

Bake the fish in a preheated moderate oven, 350°F/180°C/Gas Mark 4 (bottom right oven in a 4-door Aga), for 10 minutes. Check it to see that it is done, and if not return it to the oven for 5 minutes. (If the pieces of halibut are thicker than 1 in/2 cm, allow 20 minutes' cooking time before checking for doneness.) Meanwhile, reheat the sauce very gently: if it bubbles furiously for any length of time the vivid watercress colour will become dull. Serve the fish on warmed plates, with a spoonful of the sauce either beside or, much prettier, over half of each piece of fish.

Baked cod (or hake) with spiced green lentils

and coriander pesto

This is a lovely combination of tastes, and a most convenient dish to make: you can do everything ahead except bake the fish. Warm the lentils through as the fish cooks. The pesto will keep in the fridge for 2–3 days. (See photograph facing page 97.)

Serves 6

for the pesto
2 cloves of garlic, skinned and chopped
2 oz/50 g pine nuts, dry-fried until light brown and cooled
2 packets fresh coriander
¼ pint/150 ml olive oil
juice of 1 lime
½ tsp salt
a good grinding of black pepper

for the Puy lentils
2 tbsp olive oil
2 onions, skinned and finely chopped
1 birdseye chilli, slit open, seeded and finely sliced
6 oz/175 g Puy lentils
1 pint/600 ml vegetable stock
½ tsp salt
a good grinding of black pepper

for the fish
6 x 6 oz/175 g pieces of filleted cod or hake
3 oz/75 g butter, cut into 6
zest and juice of 1 lime

First make the pesto: put the garlic and pine nuts into a food-processor and whiz, adding the coriander as you go. Then, in a thin, steady trickle, pour in the olive oil, continuing to whiz, the lime juice, salt and pepper. Scoop and scrape the pesto into a bowl or jar, cover it and put it into the fridge until it is required.

Next cook the lentils. Heat the oil in a large saucepan, put in the onions and chilli, and cook over a moderate heat until they are soft and beginning to turn golden. Then stir in the lentils. Pour in the stock, season with salt and pepper, and bring the liquid to a simmer.

fish and seafood

Cover the pan and cook gently until the lentils are soft and the liquid has been mostly absorbed. Cool and store in the fridge.

To prepare the fish, cover a baking tray with baking parchment. Lay on it the pieces of fish, removing any remaining bones you feel as you do so. Put a piece of butter on each fillet, sprinkle over the lime juice and cover it with another piece of baking parchment.

· ·

When you want to cook the fish, bake it in a preheated moderate oven, 350°F/180°C/Gas Mark 4 (bottom right oven in a 4-door Aga), for 10–20 minutes. The time depends on the thickness of the cod – smaller, thicker pieces need longer cooking than larger, flatter pieces. To see if it's done, gently pull apart with 2 forks the thickest bit of one piece. Warm the lentils through.

To serve, spoon some lentils on to each of 6 warmed plates. Put a piece of fish on top, and a heaped teaspoonful of coriander pesto on top of the fish.

Baked lemon sole with sautéd leeks and ginger

with tomato cream sauce

You can sauté the leeks and ginger several hours in advance, and have the lemon sole ready to pop into the oven. The sauce contains just a hint of ginger and can be put together a day ahead. This piquant dish needs only some new or very well-mashed potatoes to go with it.

Serves 6

6 x 6 oz/175 g lemon sole fillets
3 oz/75 g butter, cut into 6
3 tbsp olive oil
10 medium-sized leeks, trimmed, washed and sliced diagonally into
chunks 2 in/5 cm long
2-in/5-cm piece fresh ginger, skinned and finely sliced
½ tsp salt
a good grinding of black pepper

for the tomato cream sauce

2 tbsp olive oil
3 banana shallots, skinned and finely chopped
2 sticks celery
1-in/2.5-cm piece ginger, skinned and finely chopped
1–2 cloves of garlic, to taste, skinned and finely chopped
2 x 15-oz/400 g cans chopped tomatoes
½ tsp caster sugar
½ tsp salt
a good grinding of black pepper
¼ pint/150 ml double cream

Line a baking tray with baking parchment, and lay on it the lemon sole fillets. Put a piece of butter on each and cover with baking parchment. Put the tray into the fridge and take it out 10 minutes before it will go into the oven.

For the sautéd leeks and ginger, heat the olive oil in a sauté pan and, over a moderate heat, cook the leeks and ginger, stirring carefully from time to time, until they are soft. Season with salt and pepper and take the pan off the heat. Cover it, and set it aside, or keep it in a cool place, until you are ready to reheat it.

fish and seafood

Make the creamy tomato sauce: heat the oil in a saucepan, put in the shallots and celery and cook for about 5 minutes, or until they are soft. Then add the ginger and garlic, and continue to cook for another minute. Stir in the tomatoes, season with sugar, salt and pepper, then simmer, with the pan uncovered, for 10 minutes. Take the pan off the heat and liquidize the contents until smooth. Cool and store in the fridge. (Don't add the cream yet.)

· ·

Put the fish into a preheated moderate oven, 350°F/180°C/Gas Mark 4 (bottom right oven in a 4-door Aga), and bake it for 10–15 minutes, depending on its thickness. Check it after 10 minutes. Warm the gingery leeks and the tomato sauce through, adding the cream to the tomato sauce.

Serve the baked lemon sole with a spoonful of the gingery leeks beside it, and either spoon over some of the sauce or hand it separately.

Rock turbot on a bed of sautéd fennel

with caper, shallot and butter sauce

You can substitute any firm-fleshed white fish for the rock turbot, but it is an excellent fish so if you see it, buy it. We tend to get stuck in the rut of using haddock, cod, monkfish or halibut and should try to diversify when the opportunity presents itself. In this recipe the fish can be prepared several hours in advance of cooking. You must use capers preserved in olive oil for the sauce. However, if you can't find them, buy the best – largest – you can, drain off the brine and immerse them in olive oil for 2 days before you use them. Fennel complements fish better than almost any other vegetable. It's aniseed taste becomes less intense when cooked, so don't be put off this dish if you are not a fennel fan.

Serves 6

6 x 5–6 oz/150–175 g fillets rock turbot, or similar
4 oz/110 g butter
2 tbsp olive oil
4 bulbs fennel, trimmed and thinly sliced
salt
freshly ground black pepper

for the sauce **4 banana shallots, skinned and finely diced**
½ pint/300 ml fish *or* vegetable stock
6 oz/175 g butter, diced
2 tbsp olive-oil-preserved capers, drained and chopped
a squeeze of lemon juice
a good grinding of black pepper

First prepare the fish by feeling with your fingertips and removing any remaining bones. Line a baking tray with baking parchment and lay the fish on it. Dot each piece with butter, about ½ oz/15 g per fillet, and cover with another piece of baking parchment. Keep it in a cool place until you want to cook it.

Heat the remaining butter and the oil together in a large sauté pan, and cook the fennel over a moderate heat until it is soft, 10–15 minutes. Season with salt and pepper and keep it warm until you are ready to serve.

fish and seafood

To make the sauce, put the shallots into a saucepan with the stock. Bring it to a simmer, and cook gently until the liquid has almost evaporated. Whisk in the butter, a little at a time, then stir in the capers, lemon juice and pepper. Set aside in a cool place.

. . . .

Bake the fish in a preheated moderate oven, 350°F/180°C/Gas Mark 4 (bottom right oven in a 4-door Aga), for 10–15 minutes. Warm the sauce and fennel through.

Serve the fish on a small mound of fennel, with a spoonful of the sauce over the top.

Stuffed fillets of whiting with salmon mousseline

and creamy vermouth sauce

Whiting is a most underrated fish and the perfect vehicle for this lovely deli-cate filling. You can substitute any other type of white fish for it, though, and we sometimes use lemon sole. The whole dish and its sauce can be made and assembled in the morning for that evening, stored in the fridge until you need to cook it. Take the fish out of the fridge and allow to come to room temperature for 20 minutes before baking it. Accompany with sugarsnap peas and sliced spring onions, if you like.

Serves 6

6 x 6-oz/175-g whiting fillets

for the mousseline
1 lb/450 g organic salmon, filleted
2 anchovies, drained
a good grinding of black pepper
¼ pint/150 ml double cream
1 large egg
1 egg white
juice of 1 lemon
3 oz/75 g butter, cut into 6

for the creamy vermouth sauce
3 banana shallots, skinned and finely chopped
¼ pint/l50 ml red vermouth
¼ pint/l50 ml fish stock *or* vegetable stock
½ pint/300 ml double cream
½ tsp salt
a good grinding of black pepper

To make the mousseline, put the salmon into a food-processor and whiz until smooth with the anchovies, pepper, cream, egg and extra white. Scrape the mixture into a bowl, cover it, and put it into the fridge.

To assemble the stuffed fillets, line a baking tray with baking parchment. Lay on it the fish, then put a good spoonful of the salmon mixture on to one half and fold over the other. Sprinkle over the lemon juice, and put a piece of butter on each fillet. Cover with a

fish and seafood

second sheet of baking parchment and put it into the fridge. This can be all done several hours in advance of cooking.

To make the sauce, put the shallots into a saucepan with the vermouth and stock, bring it to a simmer over a moderate heat and cook until the liquid has virtually disappeared. Then add the cream, and simmer again for a few minutes until the sauce has thickened. Season with salt and pepper. Cool and store in the fridge.

· ·

Bake the stuffed fillets (from room temperature) in a preheated moderate oven, 350°F/180°C/ Gas Mark 4 (bottom right oven in a 4-door Aga), for 15–20 minutes. Reheat the sauce gently. Serve the fish on warmed plates, with the sauce spooned over.

Baked sea bass

with lemon-and-thyme-dressed beans and tomatoes

I love this type of main course, where the main subject, the sea bass, is presented on its serving dish with the vegetables – the bean and tomato salad. You can serve it cold, if you like – it is every bit as good as it is hot. You can prepare and cook this in the morning for that evening – if you want the sea bass to be hot, cook it shortly before you plan to eat it.

Serves 6

6 x 6 oz/175 g fillets sea bass
olive oil
finely grated zest and juice of 1 lemon

for the bean and tomato salad

1 lb/450 g fine green beans, trimmed and cut in half
½ tsp thyme leaves
4 tbsp olive oil
finely grated zest of 1 lemon
2 tsp balsamic vinegar
½ tsp caster sugar
½ tsp salt
a good grinding of black pepper
8 ripe vine tomatoes, skinned, halved, seeded, then each half cut into 3

First prepare the salad. Steam the beans until they are just tender. Put all dressing ingredients – the olive oil, lemon zest, balsamic vinegar and seasonings – into a screw-topped jar and shake it vigorously. As soon as the beans are cooked, put them into a bowl and stir in the dressing thoroughly – as they cool, they will absorb the flavours. When they are cold, mix in the tomatoes. The vegetable part of this recipe (the beans and tomatoes) is intended to be served cooled (but cooked the same day that they are to be eaten – not left-over cold, from yesterday) with the fish, hot or cold, on top or among the vegetables.

Prepare the fish. Cover a baking tray with baking parchment and lay on it the sea bass fillets, removing any remaining bones you detect with your fingers. Smear each with olive oil, scatter over the lemon zest, and sprinkle with the juice. Cover with another sheet of

fish and seafood

baking parchment. Keep the tray in a cool place until you are ready
to bake the fish.

. . . .

Bake the fish in a preheated moderate oven, 350°F/180°C/Gas Mark
4 (bottom right oven in a 4-door Aga), for 10–15 minutes.

To serve, spoon the beans and tomatoes in their dressing on to a
serving dish and arrange the hot, freshly baked sea-bass fillets on top
of them.

If the sea bass is to be served cold, break it up among the beans
and tomatoes and drizzle over the whole lot about 3 tablespoons of
extra olive oil.

Baked fillet of salmon *en croûte*

with lemon and shallot sauce

This is a most elegant, delicious and convenient dish for a special occasion. The whole thing can be put together the day before, and baked just before serving. The sauce, too, can be made in advance. I love fresh garden peas, or lightly steamed sugarsnap peas, with it.

Serves 6

2 oz/50 g butter
4 banana shallots, skinned and finely sliced
½ cucumber, skinned, halved lengthways, seeded and diced thumbnail-size
½ tsp salt
a good grinding of black pepper
1½ lb/675 g ready-made puff pastry – Bell's *or* Saxby's
2 lb/900 g organic salmon, filleted, skinned and pinbones removed
1 egg, beaten

for the sauce
3 shallots, skinned and very finely sliced
½ pint/300 ml dry white wine
finely grated zest of 1 lemon
½ pint/300 ml double cream
½ tsp salt
a good grinding of black pepper

Melt the butter in a wide sauté pan, put in the shallots and cucumber and cook them for several minutes until the shallots are soft. Season with salt and pepper and leave them to cool.

Line a baking tray with baking parchment.

Roll out two-thirds of the pastry so that it is about 1½ in/4 cm bigger than the fish and lay it on the baking tray. Put the salmon on it and spoon over the cooled shallot and cucumber mixture. Roll the remaining pastry into an oblong and lay it over the salmon. Brush around the edges of the pastry with beaten egg, and crimp them firmly together. Slash the top of the pastry 4–5 times, and garnish, if you like, with 1 or more pastry fish. Brush the whole thing with the rest of the beaten egg. Cover with clingfilm and leave in a cool place.

Bake the fish *en croûte* in a preheated hot oven, 400°F/200°C/Gas Mark 6 (top right oven in a 4-door Aga), for 30–35 minutes, or until the pastry is well puffed up and deeply golden brown.

To make the sauce, put the shallots into a saucepan with the wine and simmer over a moderate heat until the wine has almost disappeared. Then add the lemon zest, cream, salt and pepper, and simmer, stirring, until it is as thick as you would like – about 2 minutes is usually enough.

Serve the salmon *en croûte* in slices, with a spoonful of the cream sauce poured over.

Smoked haddock (or cod) and parsley oatmeal crumble pie

This is a variation on a fish pie. All fish pies should be made with smoked fish: the flavour of white fish gets lost in a sauce and under a covering of mashed potatoes, puff pastry or crumble. Here the bacon adds depth to the fish mixture, which I love. As with potato-covered fish pies, this is simplicity itself to make, and convenient, too, because it only needs a green vegetable or a mixed-leaf salad to go with it. The fish part can be made and frozen for up to 3 weeks. The crumble can be made a day ahead then put over the thawed fish in its sauce, ready for cooking.

Serves 6

1½ lb/675 g smoked haddock (or cod), filleted
1½ pints/900 ml milk

for the crumble
3 oz/75 g day-old white or brown bread
a handful of parsley, stalks removed
2 oz/50 g butter
3 oz/75 g pinhead oatmeal
½ tsp salt

for the sauce
2 oz/50 g butter
2 banana shallots, skinned and finely chopped
4 rashers back bacon, fat removed, chopped
2 oz/50 g flour
the milk in which the fish was cooked
freshly ground black pepper
a grating of nutmeg

First, put the fish into a saucepan, cover it with the milk and bring it to a simmer. Take the pan off the heat, and let the fish cool in the milk. When it is cold strain the milk into a jug, and put the fish into an ovenproof dish.

To make the crumble, whiz the bread to crumbs with the parsley in a food-processor. Melt the butter in a sauté pan, put in the crumbs with the oatmeal and salt, and stir occasionally until the mixture is a dark golden colour. Scoop it on to kitchen paper and leave it to cool.

fish and seafood

Make the sauce: melt the butter in a saucepan, then put in the shallots and the bacon. Cook over a fairly high heat, stirring, until the shallots are soft and the bacon cooked. Then stir in the flour, and cook for a minute before adding the fish-flavoured milk, a little at a time, stirring continuously until the sauce bubbles. Take the pan off the heat and season with pepper and nutmeg. Pour the hot sauce over the fish, and mix it all together. Scatter the crumble over the top, and put in the fridge until you are ready to cook.

· ·

Reheat the pie from room temperature in a preheated moderate oven, 350°F/180°C/Gas Mark 4 (bottom right oven in a 4-door Aga), for 20–25 minutes or until the sauce bubbles around the sides of the dish. (If you have to reheat the pie straight from the fridge, allow an extra 25 minutes for it to be properly hot.)

Smoked haddock and prawn puff pastry pie

with tomato and caper salad

This is a delicious and satisfying main course, and so good with the tomato and caper salad. The capers must be preserved in olive oil: harsh vinegary brine ruins a good caper. Langoustines are also known as Dublin Bay prawns, and, once their heads are removed, are called scampi!

Serves 6

1½lb/675 g undyed smoked haddock, filleted and skinned
1½ pints/900 ml milk
2 oz/50 g butter
2 banana shallots, skinned and finely chopped
2 oz/50 g flour
8 oz/225 g prawn tails *or* whole langoustines, shelled and halved
2 tbsp chopped flat-leaf parsley
a good grinding of black pepper
a grating of nutmeg
12 oz/350 g puff pastry – Bell's or Saxby's
1 egg, beaten

for the tomato and caper salad

8 large, ripe vine tomatoes, skinned and thinly sliced
½ red onion, skinned and finely chopped
3 tsp oil-preserved capers, drained of their oil
2 tbsp olive oil
2 tsp balsamic vinegar
½ tsp caster sugar
½ tsp salt
a good grinding of black pepper

Put the smoked haddock into a saucepan and cover it with the milk. Bring it to a simmer over a moderate heat, then take the pan off and let the fish cool in the milk. Strain the milk into a jug – you need it for the sauce.

Melt the butter in a saucepan, put in the shallots and cook for 3–5 minutes, until they are soft. Stir in the flour and cook for a minute, then gradually add the fishy milk, stirring all the time until the sauce boils. Take the pan off the heat and stir in the raw prawn tails. Let the sauce cool, then stir in the flaked smoked haddock and the parsley. Season with pepper and nutmeg. Pour the mixture into an ovenproof pie dish.

Roll out the pastry to cover the dish, with an overlap of about ½ inch/l cm. Paint milk around the rim of the dish to help the pastry stick, then put the pastry over the dish, press down the edges and crimp them with a fork. Brush the surface of the pastry with beaten egg, and slash the top in several places with a sharp knife. Cover it with clingfilm and leave it in a cool place until you plan to bake it.

To prepare the tomato salad, put the tomato slices into a salad bowl and scatter over them the onion and capers. Mix together the olive oil, balsamic vinegar, sugar, salt and pepper, and pour it over the salad. You can make this 6–8 hours before serving.

· ·

Put the pie into a preheated hot oven, 400°F/200°C/Gas Mark 6 (top right oven in a 4-door Aga), for 25–30 minutes, or until the pastry is well puffed up and deeply golden. Serve with the tomato and caper salad alongside.

Crab cream tart with Parmesan pastry

Immodest though it undoubtedly sounds, we make the best crab tart in the world at Kinloch! It is deep and succulent and the pastry is rich and crisp. It is a convenient family main course for a special occasion, but we serve it as a first course to our hotel guests. The pastry can be made and baked 2–3 days in advance, providing that when it is cold it is wrapped in clingfilm and an airtight polythene bag and kept in a cool place. The quality of the crabmeat is, of course, essential, and we have the very best crabmeat here on Skye, from John Gilbertson at Isle of Skye Seafoods in our local town of Broadford (www.skye-seafood.co.uk). The quantities given here are for a main course.

Serves 6

for the pastry
4 oz/110 g butter, hard from the fridge, diced
1 tsp icing sugar
6 oz/175 g plain flour
½ tsp salt
a good grinding of black pepper
2 oz/50 g Parmesan, freshly grated

for the filling
2 large eggs
2 egg yolks
½ pint/300 ml double cream
2 tsp lemon juice
½ tsp Tabasco
½ tsp salt
a good grinding of black pepper
1 lb/450 g best-quality crabmeat, half and half white and brown

Put the pastry ingredients into a food processor and whiz until the mixture resembles fine crumbs. Press it firmly around the sides and base of a 9-in/22-cm flan dish or tin, and put it into the fridge for at least 1 hour. Bake it in a preheated moderate oven, 350°F/180°C/Gas Mark 4 (bottom right oven in a 4-door Aga), for 20–25 minutes. The pastry should just be shrinking away from the sides of the dish. Should the pastry slip down the sides, press it back up with the back of a metal spoon and bake for a further 3–5 minutes. Leave it to cool.

To make the filling, beat together the eggs and yolks, then beat in the cream, lemon juice, Tabasco, salt and pepper. Stir in the crab-meat thoroughly, and pour the mixture into the baked, cooled pastry case. Bake in a preheated moderate oven, 350°F/180°C/Gas Mark 4 (bottom right oven in a 4-door Aga), for 15–20 minutes, or until the centre of the filling is firm to touch – the centre is the last part to set.

. . . .

Serve warm, or cold, with vinaigrette-dressed mixed salad leaves.

Dill and lemon roulade

with smoked trout, grated apple and horseradish filling

This makes an excellent main course – or a first course, in which case this amount will serve 8. If you have it as a main course and the weather turns chilly, precede it with a warm or hot first course, a soup, perhaps, or Mushroom Strudel (page 20). I prefer to use hot-smoked trout, and try hard to remove as many of the tiny hair-like bones as I can. Apple and horseradish complement smoked trout, dill and lemon so well. You can make this several hours ahead.

Serves 6

for the roulade
1 pint/600 ml milk
1 onion, cut in half
2 sticks celery, washed and halved
a few peppercorns
salt
2 oz/50 g butter
2 oz/50 g flour
4 large eggs, separated
a grating of nutmeg
finely grated zest of 1½ lemons
2 tbsp chopped dill

for the filling
2 good eating apples, peeled and cored
2 tbsp lemon juice
½ pint/300 ml full-fat crème fraiche
salt
a good grinding of black pepper
1 rounded tbsp best-quality horseradish – Moniack, if possible
3 whole smoked trout, filleted

First, make the roulade. Put the milk, onion, celery, peppercorns and a teaspoon of salt into a saucepan over a moderate heat and scald the milk. Take the pan off the heat, and leave it to cool. Then strain the flavoured milk into a jug.

Line a baking tray with baking parchment, putting a dab of butter at each corner to anchor the paper neatly.

Melt the butter in a saucepan and stir in the flour. Let it cook for a minute, then gradually add the flavoured milk, stirring continuously until the sauce boils. Take the pan off the heat, and beat in the egg yolks, one at a time. Season with nutmeg and stir in the lemon zest. Let it cool, then stir in the dill.

In a clean bowl, whisk the egg whites with a pinch of salt till stiff. Using a large metal spoon, fold them thoroughly into the sauce. Pour the mixture into the lined baking tray and put it into a preheated moderate oven, 350°F/180°C/Gas Mark 4 (bottom right oven in a 4-door Aga), for 20 minutes, or until the centre feels firm to touch. Take the roulade out of the oven and let it cool, covered with a cloth. When it is cold turn it out on to a piece of baking parchment on a work surface.

Meanwhile make the filling. Grate the apples and stir them into the lemon juice. Add the crème fraiche, season with salt and pepper, then mix in the horseradish. Spread this over the roulade, cover it with the smoked trout, and roll up lengthways. Slip the roulade on to a serving plate by rolling it off the paper. Cover loosely with clingfilm until you are ready to slice and serve it.

. . . .

When you are ready to serve it, discard the clingfilm and carefully slice the roulade.

Crab with green mayonnaise salad

I love crab tart and crabcakes, but best of all I love cold crabmeat served with a very good mayonnaise. Crab is very filling, and I think it makes a better main than a first course. The perfect accompaniment is steamed new potatoes and a mixed-leaf salad. But good brown bread, warm, comes a close second to the potatoes. I use a mixture of olive oils for my mayonnaise: half the amount my best and most dense olive oil and the other half a light olive oil. This combination works better than using all of one or the other.

Serves 6

1½–2 lb/675–900 g best-quality crabmeat, white and brown

for the mayonnaise
1 large egg
1 large egg yolk
1 tsp Dijon mustard
½ tsp caster sugar
½–1 tsp salt
a good grinding of black pepper
¾ pint (450ml) olive oil (see note above)
grated zest and juice of 1 lemon
2 tsp balsamic vinegar, or to taste
4 tbsp chopped mixed herbs – e.g. flat-leaf parsley, chives and dill

Put the egg and the egg yolk into a food-processor with the mustard, sugar, salt and pepper, and whiz, adding the oil drop by drop, until you have a thick emulsion, then in a thin, steady trickle. If the mayonnaise is too thick for your liking, whiz in 2–3 tablespoons of near-boiling water. Whiz in the lemon juice and zest, and the balsamic vinegar. Scrape the mayonnaise into a serving bowl, and stir in the herbs. Cover the bowl, and put it into the fridge until you need it.

. . . .

To serve, mix together the white and brown crabmeat and pile them into a bowl, or serve them separately on a serving plate, white meat at one end, brown at the other. (The uninitiated may eschew the brown, not realizing it is the part of the crab with the best flavour. Only you know your guests.) Hand the mayonnaise separately.

fish and seafood

Tiger prawns (or langoustines)

in cream, brandy and slightly curried sauce

It is so easy to buy tiger prawns these days. All the large supermarkets that have fish counters sell them. But sweeter and more interesting are langoustines, which are not so easily found. Remember that both tiger prawns and langoustines are extremely filling, so don't be too generous with them: 6 per person is a comfortable amount for a main course, so buy 36 – by number, not weight. And, please, don't be put off by the cream in the ingredients: if you divide the quantity I suggest by the number of people the recipe is intended to serve you will see that the amount per person is negligible! You can make the sauce a day in advance. Serve with plain boiled basmati rice containing, if you like, 2 tablespoons chopped flat-leaf parsley, 1 tablespoon extra virgin olive oil and a little salt. A mixed leaf salad dressed with vinaigrette is also a good accompaniment.

Serves 6

36 tiger prawns or langoustines, in their shells

2 oz/50 g butter   *for the sauce*
2 medium onions, skinned and finely chopped
1 rounded tbsp medium-strength curry powder
1 rounded tsp flour
6 tbsp brandy
1 pint/600 ml double cream
½ tsp salt and a good grinding of black pepper

Plunge the prawns or langoustines in 2 or 3 batches into fast boiling water for 30 seconds – take great care not to overcook them. Let them cool and then shell them. Keep them in the fridge.

To make the sauce, melt the butter and cook the onions until they are soft, transparent and beginning to turn golden. Stir in the curry powder and flour. Cook for a minute, then add the brandy and the cream, and stir until the sauce bubbles. Taste and season with salt and pepper. Allow to cool, and store in the fridge.

· ·

Gently reheat the sauce with the prawns in it. The sauce will just coat the prawns: they don't swim in a mass of it. Serve hot.

Garlic and parsley prawns

This is as easy as it sounds, and takes only seconds to cook. We use prawn tails, which come shelled but raw in convenient packs from our fish merchant, John Gilbertson at Isle of Skye Seafoods. He does mail-order and his website address is www.skye-seafood.co.uk, so you can buy from him too. You could use tiger prawns, but they have to be shelled after cooking. On no account use those frozen packs of smallish pink-plastic type prawns. They are a waste of chewing. I like this dish with warm bread to mop up the delicious garlic juices, and with a roast ratatouille served on another plate.

Serves 6

6 oz/175g butter
4 cloves of garlic, skinned and chopped
2 lb/900 g shelled prawn tails
¼ pint/150 ml double cream
½ tsp salt
3 tbsp chopped flat-leaf parsley
6 lemon wedges

Melt the butter in a large sauté pan, put in the garlic and cook for a minute. Then add the prawn tails and stir them around. Pour in the cream, then scatter in the salt and the parsley. Serve almost immediately, with a lemon wedge.

fish and seafood

Squid in chilli sauce Provençale

Some people have been put off squid after an encounter with the rubbery deep-fried variety – like all shellfish, it is toughened by overcooking. Otherwise it is meltingly tender with its own delicate flavour. If you buy a large one you can tenderize the flesh by marinating it in milk for a few hours – but pat it dry on kitchen paper before you cook it. In this dish the tomato, olive oil, garlic and basil flavours, heightened by the chilli, complement it so well. Leave out the chilli if you really don't like it. You can make the sauce a day ahead, but cook the prepared squid (it doesn't take long) just before serving. Serve with basmati rice and mixed salad leaves.

Serves 6

5 tbsp olive oil
3 red onions, skinned and thinly sliced
1–2 red birdseye chillies, slit open, seeded and thinly sliced
2–3 cloves of garlic, skinned and finely chopped
2 x 15-oz/425-g cans chopped tomatoes
½ tsp sugar
½ tsp salt
a good grinding of black pepper
a handful of basil leaves, torn up
2 lb/900 g squid, weighed after cleaning and trimming (buy about 2½ lb/1.2 kg)

First make the sauce. Heat 3 tablespoons of the olive oil in a sauté pan or saucepan, put in the onions and chillies and cook until they are soft. Then add the garlic and tomatoes. Bring the mixture to a simmer and cook, with the pan uncovered, for 7–10 minutes. Season with the sugar, salt and pepper. Cool, and store in the fridge.

. . . .

Reheat the sauce, and add the basil just before serving or its flavour will diminish. To cook the squid, heat the remaining olive oil in a saucepan. When it is hot, add the squid in small amounts, and, as the squid turns opaque, scoop it into the sauce. Serve immediately.

Salad of scallops

with tarragon and mustard cream

Scallops, tied with crab, are my favourite shellfish – lobster is, for the most part, overrated: it is only delicious when it is brought straight from the sea to the pot and thence to the table. In this party recipe the scallops are dressed with a subtle sauce flavoured with tarragon and Dijon mustard. I like to serve a basmati rice salad with it, with fried almonds and plump and juicy raisins in the rice. I use scissors to cut off the small ridge of tough white muscle at the edge of each scallop. That's all the preparation they need.

Serves 6

18 king scallops, muscle trimmed off as above
olive oil
juice of 1 lemon

for the tarragon mustard cream sauce

1 whole egg
1 egg yolk
2 tbsp lemon juice
¼ pint/150 ml light olive oil
1 tbsp best Dijon mustard
1 tbsp fresh tarragon leaves
½ tsp salt
a good grinding of black pepper
½ tsp sugar
½ pint/300 ml double cream, lightly whipped

assorted salad leaves, perhaps with herbs and petals
about 1 tbsp snipped chives

To cook the scallops, preheat the oven to 350°F/180°C/Gas Mark 4. Cover a baking tray with baking parchment, and lay on it the scallops. Brush the scallops with olive oil, sprinkle with lemon juice, cover with baking parchment and bake in the moderate oven (bottom right oven in a 4-door Aga) for 10 minutes. Cool the scallops between the paper.

To make the sauce, put the egg, egg yolk and lemon juice into a food-processor and whiz, adding the olive oil drop by drop until you

fish and seafood

have an emulsion, then stop whizzing, and in a steady trickle add the mustard, tarragon, salt, pepper and sugar. Scrape into the bowl of whipped cream and fold in.

. . . .

On a large serving plate, arrange the salad leaves around the edge – they look so pretty if they incorporate herbs and petals. Either leave the scallops whole and put them on the dish, or if you prefer, slice them. Spoon over the tarragon and mustard cream and scatter on the chives. Keep the dish cool until you are ready to serve it.

Squid and scallops

with olive oil, lemon and parsley

This is a simple way to serve two delicious shellfish together. I prefer king scallops, and use scissors to cut off the small ridge of tough white muscle at the edge of each, which is all the preparation that scallops need. Squid is easily prepared but you will need to deal with it several hours ahead. If it has not been cleaned inside, look for the end of the plastic-like quill and pull gently: the insides should come out with it. Then wash inside, dry the squid with kitchen paper and slice it into rings. Soak the prepared squid in milk for several hours to tenderize it, then drain it and pat it dry.

Serves 6

2 cloves of garlic, skinned, optional
½ tsp salt
3 tbsp olive oil
1 lb/450 g squid, weighed when prepared as above (you will need to buy 1½ lb/675 g)
juice of 1 lemon
2 tbsp chopped flat-leaf parsley
18 scallops, muscle trimmed off as above

Pulp the garlic with the salt.

· ·

Heat the oil in a sauté pan, and cook the squid over a fairly high heat, stirring it almost continuously, for 2–3 minutes. Then add the garlic and salt, lemon juice and parsley. Scoop the squid on to a warmed dish. Lower the heat, put the scallops into the pan, and cook for barely 30 seconds on each side, until they are just opaque.

To serve, put a small heap of squid in the middle of each of 6 warmed serving plates, and arrange 3 scallops around the squid. Pour over the juices from the pan and serve.

Char-grilled monkfish, marinated in lime juice with chilli, red onion and coriander, with coriander and lime crème fraiche dressing (page 60)

fish and seafood

Scallops with hazelnut garlic butter

This may sound unlikely to some, but the combination of buttery garlic hazel-nuts with shellfish is sublime. Denis Woodtli, of the Rendezvous Restaurant at Breakish on Skye, inspired this recipe – we have eaten his scallops with hazelnut butter many times, and I would never have thought of combining such ingredients. Scallops are luxury food, and make the perfect main course for a celebration. I allow 3–4 king scallops per person. The exact number depends on the preceding course and the pudding that is to follow. The scallops can be trimmed of muscle, and the butter melted and the garlic and hazelnuts fried, several hours ahead of time. Reheat the garlic and hazelnut butter and cook the scallops just before eating. Serve accompanied by warm bread, or new potatoes roasted in their skins with olive oil and a dusting of paprika, and a mixed-leaf salad.

Serves 6

10–24 king scallops, muscle removed (see opposite)

8 oz/225 g butter *for the hazelnut*
4 oz/110 g hazelnuts, chopped *garlic butter*
2 fat cloves of garlic, skinned and finely chopped
½ tsp salt

Melt the butter in a large sauté pan. Add the hazelnuts, garlic and salt and cook over a moderate heat until the nuts smell toasted, about 4–5 minutes.

. . . .

Slip the prepared scallops into the hot (or reheated) butter, raise the heat a little, and cook them for barely a minute on each side. Serve with the hazelnut and garlic butter spooned over.

Baked cod with spiced green lentils and coriander pesto (page 70)

Meat and g

ame

There is something for everyone in this chapter – providing they eat meat! But it is vital to buy meat and chicken from a reliable butcher, who will tell you what he is selling you, where it has been raised and how. The cost of organic chicken is more or less double that of mass-produced chicken, but it is worth spending the extra for the vastly improved flavour alone. We use only organic birds here at Kinloch.

Game is no longer the preserve of the country-dweller. We can buy it from most supermarkets now, but a game-dealer or butcher will ensure that it is properly hung – and proper hanging is crucial to the flavour and texture of any game or meat.

Many people love duck – both the domestic and wild species – but not when it is cooked rare. I loathe rare duck myself. Duck should be roasted till the skin is crisp and the flesh tender – when duck is rare the meat is tough. Cooking is a form of tenderizing, which is something for cooks to remember. Thorough cooking will also kill any bacteria that might be lurking within your meat or game. Beef apart, I prefer all my meat to be cooked through.

There are many recipes in this chapter for one-pot dishes, such as Ham Hock and bean Casserole on page 136. There are recipes for summer – Bacon, Pea and Avocado Salad with Mint Dressing (page 128), for example, and Chicken Fillet Tonnato with Tomato and Caper Salad (page 106), my version of the classic Italian Vitello Tonnato. There are elegant dinner-party main courses and robust, heartening dishes such as Pork Ragout with Tomatoes, Cream and Cinnamon (page 138). Always use the best-quality meat you can find.

All the recipes are straightforward and convenient.

Char-grilled chicken with warm noodles

in a Thai dressing

The dressing is composed of a combination of salad vegetables, and although the flavours may lean towards Thailand, I can buy every ingredient in my local Co-op. I always maintain of any ingredient that if I can buy it on Skye, so can anyone buy it in even the most rural parts of the UK. Mind you, it does seem that our local Broadford Co-op is exceptionally good! All the vegetable preparation for this dish can be done the previous day, providing that everything is close-covered with clingfilm. The chicken can be made ready – olive-oil brushed and seasoned – and covered and kept in the fridge until 30 minutes before baking. I have given instructions for baking, but you could barbecue the chicken instead. (See photograph facing page 160.)

Serves 6

6 chicken breasts, preferably organic, with skin
2 tbsp olive oil
salt
freshly ground black pepper

for the noodles
4 oz/110 g fine egg noodles
3 tbsp olive oil
3 fat cloves of garlic, skinned and finely chopped
2-in/5-cm piece root ginger, skinned and finely chopped
2 red peppers, halved, seeded and diced
½ cucumber, skinned, halved lengthways, seeded and diced
1 tsp dried chilli flakes, optional
2 tbsp chopped coriander
2 tbsp strong (dark) soy sauce, such as Kikkoman's
1 tbsp sesame oil

Preheat the oven to 350°F/180°C/Gas Mark 4. Brush the chicken breasts with the olive oil, and season them with salt and pepper. Put them into the moderate oven (bottom right oven in a 4-door Aga) and bake until when you stick a knife into the thickest bit of one piece the juices run clear, 20–30 minutes. Take them out, put them on a board and slice each into 3, thickly on the diagonal.

Meanwhile, cook the noodles for 3 minutes in boiling water.

meat and game

While the noodles cook, heat the olive oil in a sauté pan and sauté over a high heat the garlic, ginger, peppers and cucumber for 2 minutes. Then stir in the chilli flakes, coriander and soy sauce. Drain the noodles and mix them immediately with the sesame oil. Stir the cooked noodles and sesame oil into the contents of the sauté pan, mix all together well, then tip the mixture on to a serving plate. Arrange the chicken slices on top – everything should be warm, but not hot. Serve.

Roast chicken (or pheasant)

with shallot, apple and Calvados cream sauce

Roast chicken is the main course most requested by all our children – who aren't really children any more! –when they come home. It always has been, and I reckon that if it still appeals to them it must appeal to many others too. It can easily be dressed up – and this yummy sauce can be made a day in advance and reheated to serve spooned beside the roast chicken. The Nutmeg, Ginger and Garlic Puréed Parsnips with Bacon Bits, on page 175, and the Broccoli with Breadcrumbs, Parsley and Capers, on page 167 are
Serves 6 *meltingly delicious accompaniments.*

for the sauce **2 oz/50 g butter**
4 banana shallots, skinned and finely chopped
1 tsp flour
¼ pint/150 ml chicken stock
4 tbsp Calvados
½ pint/300 ml double cream
3 best eating apples – e.g. Cox's, but never Golden Delicious –
peeled, quartered, cored, and sliced
½ tsp salt
a good grinding of black pepper

2 x 3 lb/1.35 kg chickens, preferably organic
4 oz/110 g butter
salt
freshly ground black pepper

First, make the sauce. Melt the butter in a saucepan and sauté the shallots for about 5 minutes, until they are turning golden. Stir in the flour, cook for a minute, then add the stock, stirring until it bubbles. Pour in the Calvados and the cream, then toss in the sliced apples and season with the salt and freshly ground black pepper. Simmer the sauce for 5 minutes then take it off the heat. Let it cool, then store it, covered, in the fridge, to reheat when the chickens are done and almost ready to be served.

To roast the chickens (or pheasant), preheat the oven to 400°F/ 200°C/Gas Mark 6 before your guests arrive. Line a roasting tin with baking parchment. Rub the chicken breasts with the butter and season with salt and pepper. Place the birds breast down in the tin, and roast in the hot oven (top right oven in a 4-door Aga) for 35 minutes. Then turn them over and roast breast side up, at the same temperature, for a further 15 minutes. Stick a knife into the deep point where the leg meets the body, and the juices should run clear. If they are pink-tinged, roast them for a further 5 minutes. Take the birds out of the oven, let them sit for 5 minutes, then carve them on to a warmed serving plate. Cover it loosely with foil, and keep it warm in a very low oven until you are ready to eat – up to 20 minutes. Any longer and it starts to dry out. Serve with the reheated sauce.

Chicken fillet tonnato

with tomato and caper salad

This dish will remind lovers of Italy of Vittello Tonnato, and this is my version. I can't buy veal in Skye so I substitute chicken fillets. Care is needed in cooking them, so that the meat doesn't become dry. The sauce is exceptionally good with the meat: fish and chicken are so very complementary to one another. Use capers preserved in olive oil, not brine. You will find such capers in health-food shops.

Serves 6

6 x 6 oz/175 g organic chicken fillets, trimmed of any fat

for the stock
3–4 pints/1.8–2.2 litres of water
2 sticks celery, broken
1 onion, halved
1 bulb fennel, chopped
small bunch crushed parsley stalks
1 bay leaf
½ tsp rock salt
a small handful of peppercorns

for the sauce
4 oz/110 g tinned tuna, well drained of its oil or brine
2 egg yolks
2 anchovy fillets
½ pint/300 ml extra virgin olive oil
a good grinding of black pepper
2 tbsp lemon juice
2 tsp oil-preserved capers, drained of their oil
2 tbsp chopped flat-leaf parsley

for the tomato and caper salad
8–10 vine tomatoes, washed and sliced
2 tsp capers, drained of their oil
½ medium red onion, finely diced
4 tbsp extra virgin olive oil
2 tsp balsamic vinegar
½ tsp salt
a good grinding of black pepper

Put all of the stock ingredients into a large saucepan, bring it to the boil and simmer for 20 minutes. Let it cool then strain. Return the stock to a pan, bring it to a simmer and put in the chicken fillets to poach for 20 minutes. Let them cool in the stock.

To make the sauce, put the tuna into a food-processor with the egg yolks and anchovies. Whiz, gradually adding the olive oil in a very thin trickle. Whiz in the pepper, and, lastly, the lemon juice. Taste, and adjust the seasoning – add more pepper and lemon juice, if you think it is needed. This will keep in the fridge for up to 2 days.

To prepare the salad, put the sliced tomatoes in a dish. Mix all the other ingredients together and spoon them over the tomatoes. Prepare this 3 to 4 hours ahead of serving.

· ·

When the chicken fillets are quite cold, take them out of their stock and slice them very thinly. Arrange them on a serving plate, and coat them with the sauce. Scatter the capers over the top, with the parsley. Serve with the salad.

Chicken marinated in lime and chilli

with aromatic rice

This is another easy recipe in which the chicken is marinated then baked, and served with the rice, which can be cooked and kept warm very successfully, providing that it is covered, for up to an hour in a low oven. Lightly steamed sliced green beans go well with it, or a mixed-leaf salad, dressed with vinaigrette.

Serves 6

6 chicken breasts, preferably organic, with the skin

for the marinade
½ pint/300 ml olive oil
2 cloves of garlic, skinned and finely chopped
finely grated zest of 2 limes
2 tbsp strong (dark) soy sauce, such as Kikkoman's
1 birdseye chilli, slit open, seeded and finely sliced
a good grinding of black pepper

for the rice
3 tbsp olive oil
3 banana shallots, skinned and very finely chopped
2 cloves of garlic, skinned and finely chopped
2-in/5-cm piece fresh ginger, skinned
12 oz/350 g basmati rice
2 cardamom seeds, bashed, husks removed
about 2 pints/1.2 litres chicken stock
1 tsp chopped coriander
½ tsp salt
a good grinding of black pepper

Put the chicken breasts into an ovenproof dish or roasting tin. Mix together the marinade ingredients, and pour over the chicken. Leave it for several hours, or overnight, turning the chicken occasionally.

. . . .

About an hour before guests arrive, bake the chicken in a preheated hot oven, 400°F/200°C/Gas Mark 6 (top right oven in a 4-door Aga), for 15 minutes, then lower the heat to moderate, 350°F/180°C/Gas Mark 4 (bottom right oven in a 4-door Aga), and bake for a further

meat and game

25 minutes, or until the juices run clear when the chicken is pierced with a knife, and the skin is crisp. Keep the chicken warm in a very low oven until you are ready to eat.

Meanwhile, prepare the rice: heat the olive oil in a saucepan and sauté the shallots, garlic and ginger until the shallots are soft. Stir in the rice, so that each grain is coated with oil, over a fairly high heat. Add the cardamom, and pour in the stock until it comes about 1 in/2.5 cm above the level of the rice. Beware: the stock will cause a whoosh of steam as it is poured onto the rice. Do not stir at all after you have added the stock: cover the pan with a folded tea-towel, then with the lid on and, over a gentle heat, leave it to cook for 5 minutes. Draw the pan off the heat and leave it for 15 minutes. Do not, on any account, lift the lid and the cloth until the 15 minutes are up, when the rice will have absorbed the stock. Keep it warm in a low oven until you need it.

Just before serving, stir the coriander, salt and pepper into the rice. Serve with the warm chicken breasts.

Chicken, mushroom and shallot pie

with almond oatmeal butter crust

This is a pie with a difference: it has no pastry or potato on top. Instead, it has a crisp almond and oatmeal crust, utterly delicious with the creamy mushroom and chicken filling. The flaked almonds and oatmeal are fried in butter until golden before being put on top of the creamy chicken and mushroom mixture, which is spiked with lemon to enhance its taste still further: I don't think you'll need potatoes with it, but a purée of root vegetables and, perhaps, a mixed leaf salad would set it off beautifully. The

Serves 6 *pie can be made a couple of days ahead.*

1 x 3½–4 lb/2 kg chicken, preferably organic
1 onion, halved, skin left on
1 stick celery
2 tsp black peppercorns
1 lb/450 g mushrooms, wiped and chopped
2 tbsp olive oil
1 tsp salt
2 oz/50 g butter
6 banana shallots, skinned and sliced
1½ oz/40 g flour
½ pint/300 ml double cream
finely grated zest of 1 lemon
a good grinding black of pepper
a grating of nutmeg

for the top **3 oz/75 g butter**
4 oz/110 g flaked almonds
4 oz/110 g pinhead oatmeal
2 tsp salt

Put the chicken into a large saucepan with the onion, celery and peppercorns. Cover it with water, put a lid on the pan and bring it to a gentle simmer. Cook it for 1 hour, or until when you stick a knife into the thickest part of the thigh the juices run clear. If they are tinged pink, simmer for a further 10 minutes. Let the cooked chicken cool in its stock. Then lift it out and strip the meat from the carcass. Strain the stock through a sieve into a large jug or bowl, and measure out 1 pint/600 ml for the sauce.

Preheat the oven to 400°F/200°C/Gas Mark 6.

Line a baking tray with baking parchment. Put the mushrooms on this, and rub the olive oil into them with your hands. Sprinkle over the salt, and roast them in the hot oven (top right oven in a 4-door Aga) for 20 minutes. Then shuffle them around, and continue to roast for 10 minutes. They will absorb scarcely any oil as they roast, whereas if you fry or sauté them they soak up oil like blotting paper.

Melt the butter in a large saucepan or sauté pan, add the shallots, and sauté them for 5 minutes, or until they are very soft. Stir in the flour, and let the mixture cook for a minute. Pour in the stock and stir until the sauce bubbles. Add the cream, stir, and let the sauce boil again. Take the pan off the heat, stir in the lemon zest, pepper and nutmeg and the mushrooms. Let the contents of the pan cool, then stir in the chicken. Put the mixture into an ovenproof dish.

Make the top: melt the butter in a sauté pan, and put in the flaked almonds, oatmeal and salt. Stir this all around over a moderately high heat until the almonds and oatmeal turn golden brown. Spoon it evenly over the chicken and mushroom mixture. Store the pie in the fridge until you need it.

. . . .

Let the pie come to room temperature for 30 minutes before reheating in a preheated moderate oven, 350°F/180°C/Gas Mark 4 (bottom right oven in a 4-door Aga), for 35–45 minutes, until the sauce is bubbling gently and the top is sizzling. Serve.

Chicken braised in white wine

This is very much more interesting than it sounds, a richly creamy and spicy treat. The finished dish keeps warm satisfactorily for up to an hour in a low oven. I like to serve it with lightly steamed sugarsnap peas, and either well-mashed potatoes or boiled basmati rice. Prepare the dish up to a day in advance, then reheat gently to serve.

Serves 6

3 tbsp olive oil
6 chicken breasts, with skin
4 banana shallots, skinned and very finely chopped
1 tsp flour
2 tsp medium curry powder
½–1 tsp dried chilli flakes, to taste
½ pint/300 ml dry white wine
½ pint/300 ml double cream
½ tsp salt
a good grinding of black pepper

Heat the olive oil in a sauté pan (which has a lid) and cook the chicken breasts until the skin is golden brown. Brown them briefly on the other side, then remove them to a warm dish. Add the shallots to the pan, and cook them over a medium heat until they are very soft and turning golden. Stir in the flour, curry powder and chilli flakes and cook for a minute, then pour in the white wine. Stir until it bubbles, add the cream and stir until it bubbles again. Then put in the chicken breasts, season with salt and pepper, cover the pan with its lid and, over a very gentle heat, simmer for 15 minutes, or until the juices run clear when you stick a knife into a thick bit of chicken. If it is tinged pink, cover the pan again and simmer gently for a few more minutes. Cool, cover and keep the pan in the fridge.

. . . .

Reheat gently – not fast – then simmer for 15 minutes. Serve.

Rabbit casseroled with shallots, apples and cider

Rabbit is a delicious alternative to chicken, and easily bought these days, oven ready, if you don't shoot your own. You can, of course, use chicken instead of rabbit in this recipe if you prefer. The cream is optional, but it makes all the difference to the finished dish. You can make it a day in advance, but don't add the cream until you reheat it. Serve with either baked jacket or mashed potatoes, and courgettes stir-fried with garlic.

Serves 6

2 tbsp flour
2 tsp salt
a good grinding of black pepper
6 x 5-oz/150 g rabbit joints
3 tbsp olive oil
6 banana shallots, skinned and finely chopped
4 good eating apples, e.g. Cox's, peeled, cored and sliced
1 pint/600 ml dry cider, or unsweetened apple juice
½ pint/300 ml double cream, optional

Preheat the oven to 350°F/180°C/Gas Mark 4.

Put the flour into a polythene bag with the salt and pepper and shake it. Then add the rabbit joints and shake to coat them in the seasoned flour. Heat the oil in a large ovenproof sauté pan or casserole and brown the rabbit on both sides. Remove it to a warm dish. Sauté the shallots until they are very soft and beginning to turn golden at the edges, then add the apples and the cider, and stir carefully – so that you do not break up the apple slices – until the sauce boils. Replace the rabbit in the pan, spooning the apple and shallots over it, and when the liquid is simmering once more, put on the lid. Put the pan into the moderate oven (bottom right oven in a 4-door Aga), for 45 minutes. Take it out, allow it to cool and store it in the fridge.

. . . .

To reheat the casserole, bring it to room temperature for 30 minutes, then on the hob bring the liquid to a simmer, and pour in the cream. Simmer gently for 20 minutes, with the pan covered. Serve.

Roast duck with orange mustard sauce

Roast duck is too often overlooked as a main course, which is a shame. Gressingham (or, indeed, Goosnargh) ducks are now fairly widely available. Do buy either type if you can – their flavour is more interesting than that of the average domestic duck. And a fresh duck is better still than a frozen duck. Many cooks are wary of serving duck because they are not sure how many one duck will feed. Perhaps they have discovered on carving that the breastbone is shallow and that a large bird yields little meat. The easiest way to tackle a roast duck is to quarter it. This isn't difficult if you have a sturdy pair of sharp scissors. There are several convenient sauces or relishes that complement the richness of a roast duck, and this one could not be simpler, or more delicious: it can also be made in advance. The crisp roast duck can be quartered and kept warm – uncovered – in a low oven for up to 45 minutes. I like to serve it with Puréed Peas with Shallots and Mint (page 174), and steamed or boiled new potatoes. This serves 6 with 2 quarters to

Serves 6 *eat cold the next day – a delicious bonus. (See photograph facing page 129.)*

2 x 3½ lb/1.5 kg domestic *or* Gressingham ducks

for the sauce **pared rind and juice of 2 oranges, rind sliced into thin strips**
1 x 1 lb/450 g jar jellied marmalade
2 tbsp lemon juice
1 tbsp best Dijon mustard

Start by making the sauce – a couple of days in advance, if you like. Poach the strips of orange rind in simmering water for 15 minutes, then drain in a sieve. Put the marmalade into a saucepan with the lemon and orange juice. Stir over a moderate heat until it has melted. Then stir in the Dijon mustard, take the pan off the heat and either store the sauce in the fridge until you are ready to use it, or set it aside to reheat when you are about to serve the duck.

Before guests arrive, roast the ducks. Preheat the oven to 400°F/ 200°C/Gas Mark 6, and line the base of a fairly deep roasting tin with foil. Dry inside each duck with a wodge of kitchen paper and put them into the tin. Cover them with a sheet of baking parchment until you are ready to roast them. Remove the paper covering, and roast them in the hot oven (top right oven in a 4-door Aga) for 1 hour 20 minutes. To serve, take a very sharp, heavy pair of scissors and cut down either side of the backbone. Then cut across, behind each leg. This will give you 4 neat quarters, without the backbone. If you like,cut off each leg at the top knuckle. Keep warm in a low oven.

. . . .

Serve with some of the reheated orange mustard sauce spooned over each duck quarter.

Roast duck with onion and orange confiture

Here is another roast duck recipe – another, because I think we should eat duck more often. The Onion and Orange Confiture can be made several days in advance and is just as good with roast wild duck as it is with a roast domestic bird. Serve the duck cut into quarters, not carved. As with the preceding recipe, this recipe serves 6 with 2 duck quarters to eat cold the next day.

Serves 6

2 x 3½-lb/1.5-kg domestic *or* Gressingham ducks

for the **2 sweet oranges**
confiture **3 tbsp olive oil**
6 red onions, skinned and very thinly sliced
2 tsp Demerara sugar
2 tsp salt
1 tbsp lemon juice
2 tsp Tabasco

First make the confiture. Wash the oranges thoroughly under running water, then halve and slice them as thinly as you can. Put the slices into a saucepan and cover them with cold water, bring it to a simmer and cook for 25 minutes. Check that the water doesn't evaporate, and top it up if necessary. The thickest part of the peel should be very soft at the end of the cooking time. Drain the orange slices, and leave them to cool.

Meanwhile, heat the olive oil in a large saucepan or sauté pan, and cook the onions over a moderate heat, stirring from time to time, for 35–40 minutes. During this time stir in the Demerara sugar and salt. Once the onions start caramelizing, stir in the lemon juice, the Tabasco, and the orange slices. Cook over a moderate heat for a further 10 minutes. Reheat to serve.

Before guests arrive, roast the ducks. Preheat the oven to 400°F/200°C/Gas Mark 6, and line the base of a fairly deep roasting tin with foil. Dry inside each duck with a wodge of kitchen paper and put them into the tin. Cover them with a sheet of baking parchment until you are ready to roast them. Remove the paper covering, and roast them in the hot oven (top right oven in a 4-door Aga) for 1 hour 20 minutes. To serve, take a very sharp, heavy pair of scissors and cut down either side of the backbone. Then cut across, behind each leg. This will give you 4 neat quarters, without the backbone. If you like,cut off each leg at the top knuckle. Keep warm in a low oven.

. . . .

Serve with some of the confiture alongside each duck quarter.

Meatballs in sour cream sauce

Meatballs are utterly delicious – but only if they are made with a combination of the finest beef, minced, and the best pork sausagemeat or minced belly pork. This, for me, is made by Duncan Fraser, our butcher in Inverness, who is beyond betterment. People of all ages love meatballs, and they are worthy of a dinner party when served in this sour cream sauce. (They are also just as good served in a rich tomato and chilli sauce, such as that on page 16, and they freeze very well in this too, though they do not freeze so well in the soured cream sauce.) Make this dish up to 2 days in advance and keep it in the fridge.

Serves 6

for the meatballs
1½ lb/675 g rump steak, trimmed of fat and minced
1½ lb/675 g best quality pork sausages, skinned, or minced belly pork
4 banana shallots, skinned and very finely chopped
3 tbsp chopped parsley
2 tsp salt
a good grinding of black pepper
1 large egg, beaten well
a plateful of sieved plain flour
2 tbsp olive oil, or other oil if preferred, for frying the meatballs

for the sauce
2 oz/50 g butter
2 shallots, skinned and very finely chopped
1 pint/600 ml chicken stock
juice of 1 lemon
¾ pint/450 ml double cream
½ tsp salt
a good grinding of black pepper
1 tsp best horseradish sauce

First, make the meatballs. Put the minced steak and skinned sausages into a bowl with the shallots, parsley, salt, pepper and beaten egg. With your hands – there is no other way to do this – squelch the ingredients together until everything is thoroughly combined. Then shape the mixture into golf balls, as even in size as

meat and game

possible, and roll each well in flour. Heat the olive oil in a large sauté pan, to a depth of about ½ inch/1 cm, and fry the meatballs, turning them over and over so they brown and cook evenly, 5–7 minutes. You may need to do this in batches. As they are cooked, lift them on to a large dish lined with a couple of thicknesses of kitchen paper to absorb excess oil. When they are all done put them into a wide oven-proof dish.

To make the sauce, melt the butter in a wide saucepan or sauté pan and cook the finely chopped shallots for 4–5 minutes until they are soft. Pour in the stock, bring it to the boil, then simmer until the liquid has reduced by half. Add the lemon juice, then the cream, salt, pepper and horseradish, and continue to simmer until the sauce has thickened to the consistency of thick pouring cream. Pour it over the meatballs. Let it cool, then keep it in the fridge until you need it.

. . . .

To reheat the dish, cover it with baking parchment (*not* foil), bring it to room temperature for about 30 minutes then put it into a pre-heated moderate oven, 350°F/180°C/Gas Mark 4 (bottom right oven in a 4-door Aga), for 30 minutes or until the sauce bubbles gently around the meatballs. Let it simmer for another 5–10 minutes, then serve.

Lamb curry Maldives-style

This rather loosely named recipe is the result of our eldest daughter Alexandra and her husband Philipp's description of a dish they ate for dinner one evening in the Maldives on their honeymoon. They enjoyed it so much that Alexandra got the recipe – sort of – from the chef, and has since made it on several occasions in Salzburg, where they live. You can substitute chicken for the lamb, but whichever you use it will be truly delicious. If you use lamb, shoulder is the sweetest cut for this, but you can use leg if you prefer. You can make the curry and the relish a day in advance. Serve with

Serves 6   *plain boiled basmati rice.*

3 tbsp olive oil

2 lb/900 g lamb, weighed when trimmed, cut into l-in/2.5-cm chunks
  (buy 2½ lb/1.1 kg)

2 tsp each cumin seeds

2 tsp coriander seeds

1 tsp cardamom seeds

6 banana shallots, skinned and finely chopped

2 fat cloves of garlic, skinned and finely chopped

2-in/5-cm piece root ginger, skinned and finely chopped

½ tsp ground cloves

1 level tsp cornflour

½ pint/300 ml chicken *or* vegetable stock

6 ripe vine tomatoes, skinned and chopped – seeds and all

1 x l5-oz/425-g tin coconut milk

½ tsp salt

for the   1 cucumber, skinned, halved lengthways, seeded and diced
cucumber   ½ pint/300 ml thick full-fat natural yoghurt
relish   2 tbsp chopped coriander
            ½ tsp salt
            a grinding of black pepper

Preheat the oven to 300°F/150°C/Gas Mark 3.

Heat the oil in a sauté pan or casserole dish and brown the lamb, a small amount at a time. Remove it to a warm dish. Meanwhile, bash the cumin, coriander and cardamom together in a mortar with a pestle – discard the cardamom husks. When the lamb is all browned, put the shallots, garlic and ginger into the pan and sauté over moderate heat until the shallots are beginning to turn golden brown, then stir in the pounded spices and the ground cloves, and cook, stirring, for a further minute.

Mix the cornflour with a little of the stock, then add it with the tomatoes, the rest of the stock and the coconut milk, and stir until it is simmering. Replace the browned lamb in the pan, bring it back to a simmer, season with salt, cover and put the curry into the pre-heated low moderate oven (bottom of the bottom right oven in a 4-door Aga) for 1–1¼ hours. Meanwhile make the relish: put the cucumber into a bowl with the yoghurt, coriander, salt and pepper. Mix all together thoroughly, cover the bowl and keep it in the fridge till you are ready to serve.

Take the pan out of the oven, cool, and store it in the fridge.

. . . .

To reheat the curry, take it into room temperature for 30 minutes, then bring it to a simmer on the hob, and continue to *simmer very gently* for a minimum of 10 minutes – fast boiling will destroy the texture of the dish. Serve with the relish alongside.

Baked spare ribs

in barbecue sauce

We hadn't eaten spare ribs for about twenty-five years until a recent visit to Berlin, where they were served at an informal party. They were delicious, and fun to eat. Spare ribs can only be eaten held in the fingers – messy, but so good. A supply of paper table napkins is an essential accompaniment to a dish of spare ribs with barbecue sauce! The ribs need long and fairly slow cooking – it's almost impossible to overcook a spare rib – so they are especially convenient because you can put them into the oven and pretty much forget about them. I like to serve them with baked jacket potatoes, or better still, a dish of cannellini beans dressed with olive oil, garlic and parsley – and chilli too if, like us, you are a chilli addict. You need to marinate the ribs the night before cooking them.

Serves 6

3 racks of ribs

for the marinade
¼ pint/150 ml strong soy sauce
½ pint/300 ml olive oil
3 tbsp sesame oil
3 fat garlic cloves, skinned and finely chopped
1 tbsp dark brown *or* molasses sugar
2-in/5-cm piece root ginger, skinned and finely chopped

for the barbecue sauce
2 red onions, skinned and very thinly sliced
½ pint/300 ml of the reserved marinade
2 x 15-oz/425-g tins chopped tomatoes
2 cloves of garlic, skinned and finely chopped
2 tbsp Heinz tomato ketchup – *only* Heinz will do

Lay the ribs in a wide roasting tin. Mix together all the ingredients for the marinade and pour it over them. Leave them overnight, but turn the ribs before you go to bed and before you cook them.

To bake the ribs, preheat the oven to 350°F/180°C/Gas Mark 4. Drain off the marinade – reserve ½ pint/300 ml for the sauce – and put the roasting tin into the moderate oven (bottom right oven in a 4-door Aga), for 40 minutes, then lower the heat to slow,

250°F/125°C/Gas Mark ½, and bake for a further 2 hours (top left oven in a 4-door Aga).

To make the sauce, put the onions with the reserved marinade into a saucepan and cook over a moderate heat until the onions are very soft – if the heat is too high the sugar in the marinade will burn. Then add the tomatoes, garlic and ketchup, and simmer for 10 minutes. Set aside while the ribs finish cooking.

. . . .

Serve the spare ribs hot from the oven with the sauce (reheated if necessary) alongside.

Marinated fillet steaks with avocado salsa

and baked potatoes with mustard cream

This is a most convenient main course for a celebratory dinner. The steaks can be marinated a day ahead, needing only to be patted dry and seared before eating. The salsa is full of flavour and texture: it's a chunky one, and doubles up as the vegetable accompaniment. You can make the salsa a day ahead too, but don't add the avocado until shortly before you need it. And the mustard cream dresses up the baked potatoes wonderfully and is much more interesting than just butter. I like Dijon mustard best of the lot, but you might prefer English, grainy or German sweet mustard. Use whichever appeals most to you.

Serves 6

6 x 5–6 oz/150–175 g fillet steaks, trimmed of fat and membrane

for the marinade

6 tbsp olive oil
3 cloves of garlic, skinned and thinly sliced
2 tsp black peppercorns, bashed with a pestle in a mortar
1 tbsp strong (dark) soy sauce

for the avocado salsa

8 ripe vine tomatoes, skinned, seeded and diced thumbnail-size
2 red onions, skinned and very finely diced
2 sticks celery, washed, trimmed and very thinly sliced
1 birdseye chilli, slit open, seeded and very thinly sliced, optional
3 tbsp olive oil
2 tsp balsamic vinegar
½ tsp salt
2 tbsp chopped coriander
4 large *or* 6 smaller avocados

for the mustard cream

½ pint/300 ml double cream, loosely whipped
2 tbsp snipped chives
2 tbsp lemon juice
1–2 tbsp Dijon mustard

for the baked potatoes

6 baking potatoes, scrubbed
olive oil and crushed sea salt

meat and game

Mix together the marinade ingredients. Put the steaks into a wide dish and spoon over the marinade. Leave it in a cool place for several hours or, best of all, overnight. Turn the steaks in the marinade once or twice.

To make the salsa, mix together all the ingredients except the avocado. Keep the bowl covered, in the fridge.

Stir together all the ingredients for the mustard cream, cover the bowl, and leave it in the fridge overnight. On the day of serving, pre-heat the oven to 400°F/200°C/Gas Mark 6. Rub the potatoes with olive oil, roll them in the sea salt then bake them in the hot oven (top right oven in a 4-door Aga) for 50–60 minutes.

. . . .

About 3 hours before serving, you can skin, halve, stone and dice the avocado and add it to the salsa. Closely cover the bowl so that the avocado does not discolour.

To cook the steaks, lift them out of the marinade and pat them dry with kitchen paper. Heat a griddle and, when it is very hot, sear the steaks, resisting the temptation to turn them for 1 minute. Cook them on each side for 1 minute for medium rare, longer if you like your meat medium cooked, and for a little less time if you like it rare.

Serve the steaks with the salsa, and the baked jacket potatoes with the mustard cream handed separately.

Pasta with pork Bolognese

Providing you use the best-quality pork sausages or minced belly pork, this is the most delicious variation on a beef Bolognese sauce. It was inspired by a pasta dish we ate on a family holiday in Umbria. My son-in-law, who adored it, soon regretted raving about how good it was, because suddenly our forks were all in his plate. A warning: it's filling! You can make the sauce a couple of days in advance – keep it in a covered bowl in the fridge. The minced belly pork is rather a new discovery of mine. It is well worth trying as an alternative to sausagemeat.

Serves 6

for the sauce
3 tbsp olive oil
2 onions, skinned and finely chopped
2 cloves of garlic, skinned and finely chopped
2 lb/900 g best-quality pork sausages, skinned, *or* minced belly pork
3 tbsp tomato purée
a sprig of thyme, leaves only
finely grated zest of 1 lemon
½ tsp caster sugar
½ tsp salt and a good grinding of black pepper
1 pint/600 ml red wine

1 lb/450 g pasta, such as spaghetti or tagliatelle
3 tbsp extra virgin olive oil
freshly grated Parmesan, to serve

Heat the olive oil in a heavy-based saucepan or sauté pan, put in the onions and cook until they are beginning to turn golden brown. Add the garlic and the sausages and continue to cook, breaking up the sausages with the side of your wooden spoon until there are no lumps, for about 5 minutes. Stir in the tomato purée, the thyme, lemon zest, seasonings and wine, then let it simmer very gently for 20–25 minutes, with the pan covered. Remove the lid, and simmer uncovered for a further 5–10 minutes. Allow to cool, then store in the fridge in a covered bowl until you are ready to reheat it.

meat and game

Bring a large pan of water to a rolling boil, add salt and then add the pasta, and cook until the pasta is just tender (but still has a little bite to it).

Meanwhile, reheat the sauce.

Drain the pasta thoroughly, mix in the extra virgin olive oil and serve with the sauce and freshly grated Parmesan.

Bacon, pea and avocado salad

with mint dressing

One day last summer, with an unexpected lunchtime visit from cousins and with little in the larder but a large quantity of peas in the pod, I came up with this salad. It was surprisingly good. However, I have never made it with frozen peas: freshly shelled peas have a lovely earthy quality, which, much as I love them, frozen peas lack and which this dish needs. It is effortless to make, but won't keep more than an hour or so – and not at all after the avocado is added. Serve the salad surrounded by leaves with some warmed bread.

Serves 6

12 rashers smoked back bacon
1½ lb/675 g shelled fresh peas, weighed after shelling
4 ripe avocados

for the dressing
6 tbsp olive oil
1 tbsp balsamic vinegar
1 tsp caster sugar
½ tsp salt
a good grinding of black pepper
finely grated zest of 1 lemon
2 tbsp finely chopped applemint

If you cook in an Aga, line a roasting tin with baking parchment and lay the bacon on it. Put the tin in the hottest oven and cook till crisp. Alternatively, grill the bacon until crisp. Lay the rashers on kitchen paper to soak up the fat, and when they are cool enough to handle, break them into a large salad bowl.

Steam the peas until they are just tender, then tip them into the bowl.

While the peas are steaming, mix together all of the dressing ingredients and pour it immediately over the steamed peas in the bowl – as they cool, the peas will absorb all the flavours. Set aside.

. . . .

Peel the avocados, flick out the stones and dice the flesh. Carefully mix the avocados into the peas, bacon and dressing, and serve.

Ham hock and bean casserole (page 136)

meat and game

Pork fillet with lemon, cream and capers

This is a luxurious dish for a special occasion. It will only be delicious if the capers are preserved in olive oil, not in brine. Try making it with a Seville orange, when they are in season, instead of the lemon. It can be made ahead and reheated, but it does not freeze successfully. I like well-mashed potatoes with this, and a green vegetable such as sliced green beans.

Serves 6

2 lb/900 g pork fillets, trimmed of membrane
2–3 tbsp olive oil
4 banana shallots, skinned and very finely chopped
½ pint/300 ml chicken stock
finely grated zest of 2 lemons, each washed and dried first, and the juice of 1
2 heaped tsp oil-preserved capers, drained
½ pint/300 ml double cream
½ tsp salt
a good grinding of black pepper

Slit the pork fillets lengthways and bash them flat between 2 pieces of baking parchment. Cut each fillet in half. Heat the olive oil in a large sauté pan and, over a moderate heat, brown the pieces of pork fillet on either side – you will almost certainly need to do this in two batches. Remove them to a serving dish and keep them warm. If you need to, add another tablespoon of oil to the pan, stir in the shallots and cook until they are soft, 3–5 minutes, stirring, then add the stock, lemon zest and juice, and the capers. Simmer until the stock has reduced by about half, then stir in the cream, salt and pepper. Let it bubble for 2–3 minutes, then pour it over the pork fillet. Cover the dish – not with foil – and let it cool.

. . . .

Reheat the pork in a preheated moderate oven at 350°F/180°C/ Gas Mark 4 (bottom right oven in a 4-door Aga), until the sauce simmers around the meat, then continue to simmer, very gently, for 10 minutes to heat the meat safely through. Serve.

Roast duck with orange mustard sauce (page 114)

Soy and ginger marinated pork fillets

with leek and ginger cream sauce

This is a most convenient main course, because the pork can be marinated for up to 2 days, and takes only minutes to sauté. The sauce can be made a day in advance, and has the added advantage of being a vegetable and a sauce in one. The fragrant smells of the combined leeks, ginger, garlic and soy sauce develop into a most delicious tasting dish, with a creamy texture. Roast root vegetables are the perfect accompaniment for this dish, or, quite the opposite, steamed sugarsnap peas (whose crunch I love). Plain boiled basmati rice with chopped parsley forked through is also perfect, and rice keeps warm in a cool oven until you need it: but don't be tempted to add the parsley until just before you serve it.

Serves 6

½ pint/300 ml olive oil, plus a little extra
½ pint/300 ml best soy sauce – Superior Soy, Kikkoman's *or* Kicap Manis
2 cloves of garlic, skinned and sliced
2-in/5-cm piece root ginger, skinned and sliced
2 lb/900 g pork fillet, trimmed of membrane and cut into 1 in/2.5 cm thick slices

for the leek and ginger sauce

3 tbsp olive oil
10 leeks, trimmed, washed and sliced about 1 in/2.5 cm thick
2-in/5-cm piece root ginger, skinned and finely chopped
½ pint/300 ml double cream

You will see that there is no salt in this recipe – the soy sauce adds enough saltiness to both the marinade and the sauce. First, make the marinade: put the olive oil, soy sauce, garlic and ginger into a saucepan and bring it to a simmer, then cook for 1 minute. Take it off the heat and let it cool.

Put the pork fillet slices into a wide, shallow dish, and pour over the cold marinade. Cover, and leave it in a cool place for a minimum of 8 hours, turning the pieces of pork once. If you marinate the pork for longer, turn the slices more often.

To make the sauce, heat the olive oil in a sauté pan and sauté the leeks and ginger over a moderate heat, stirring occasionally, until the leeks are very soft. They should not be allowed to colour. Pour off

meat and game

¼ pint/150 ml of the pork's marinade, add it to the sauce and let it simmer for a minute. Stir in the cream, and simmer again until the sauce is thick – about 2 minutes. Allow to cool, and leave in the fridge. The pork can continue to steep in the remainder of the marinade.

. . . .

When you are ready to cook the pork, pat it dry on kitchen paper. Heat some olive oil in a frying pan. Sauté the pork for 2–3 minutes on each side, then put it into a warm ovenproof serving dish. Keep it in a low oven until you are ready to serve with the reheated sauce.

Pork fillet with spinach, mushrooms and Parmesan

Serves 6

This dish can be prepared several hours in advance and takes only minutes to finish off. As it contains spinach, it needs only potatoes to accompany it – try them roasted in olive oil.

1½ lb/675 g mushrooms, field, if possible, wiped and chopped
5 tbsp olive oil
2 lb/900 g pork fillet, trimmed of any membrane, cut into ½-in/1 cm thick slices
6 oz/175 g baby spinach leaves
½ pint/300 ml dry white wine
½ tsp salt
a good grinding of black pepper
3 oz/75 g fresh bread
1 oz/25 g parsley
2 oz/50 g butter
2 oz/50 g freshly grated Parmesan

Preheat the oven to 400°F/200°C/Gas Mark 6. Rub an ovenproof dish with olive oil.

Line a baking tray with baking parchment, and put the chopped mushrooms on it. Rub 2 tablespoons of the olive oil into them, then roast them in the hot oven (top right oven in a 4-door Aga), for 25–30 minutes, shuffling them around once during their cooking time.

Meanwhile, heat 2 tablespoons of olive oil in a sauté pan, and sauté the pork fillet, a few slices at a time, until browned on either side. Remove them to a dish. When they are all done, add the remaining tablespoon of olive oil to the pan, and put in the spinach leaves, season them with a grating of nutmeg, clap on the lid and cook for 2 minutes. Put the spinach into the oiled ovenproof dish. Lay the browned pork fillet slices on top, cover the dish and set it aside.

Put the roasted mushrooms into a saucepan with the white wine. Simmer them gently, with the pan uncovered, for 5 minutes – the wine should reduce to a syrupy texture. Season, then pour this over the pork and spinach.

meat and game

Whiz the bread in a food-processor with the parsley. Melt the butter in a frying pan, then sauté the parsley breadcrumbs, stirring, until the crumbs are golden brown. Spoon them over the mushrooms, then scatter the Parmesan over the top. Set aside for a few hours.

. . . .

Put the dish under a hot grill until the Parmesan melts. Then put the dish into a preheated moderate oven, 350°F/180°C/Gas Mark 4 (bottom right oven in a 4-door Aga), for 20 minutes, until it has small simmering bubbles around the edges. Serve.

Spiced braised pork

Pork shoulder makes an excellent casserole. It's lean and tender, and such a good cut of meat that I'm surprised we don't use it more. The spices in this recipe impart a delicate flavour and mouthwatering smell to the dish, and the chilli gives it a gently fiery kick. As with many casseroles it improves with being made the day before you need it, and the meat, potatoes and vegetables are all in one dish – a boon, especially when it comes to washing up.

Serves 6

2 tbsp flour

2 tsp salt

a good grinding of black pepper

2 lb/900 g pork shoulder, weighed when trimmed of fat, cut into 1-in/2.5-cm chunks

4 tbsp olive oil – you may need more

4 onions, skinned and thinly sliced

1–2 cloves of garlic, skinned and finely chopped

½ tsp dried chilli flakes, *or* ½ birdseye chilli, seeded and thinly sliced

1 tsp saffron strands

½ tsp ground cinnamon

¼ tsp ground cloves

2 pints/1.2 litres good stock, *either* beef, vegetable *or* chicken

6 medium potatoes, peeled and cut into 1-in/2.5-cm chunks

finely grated zest of 1 lemon

3 oz/75 g cashew nuts, chopped

6 ripe vine tomatoes, skinned, halved, seeded, and each half cut into 3

3 tsp soft brown sugar

Preheat the oven to 300°F/150°C/Gas Mark 3.

Put the flour into a polythene bag with the salt and pepper and shake vigorously to mix it. Then add the pork and shake again to coat each chunk. Heat the oil in a heavy sauté pan or casserole, put in the meat and brown it well on all sides – you may need to do this in batches. Remove each browned batch, with a slotted spoon, to a warm dish. Then lower the heat a little, add another tablespoon of oil, if you think it is needed, put in the onions and cook them until they are very soft and beginning to turn golden, about 5 minutes. Stir

meat and game

in the garlic and the spices, cook for 30 seconds then pour in the stock and stir until the liquid is simmering. Then add the potatoes and the browned meat, and heat until the liquid is simmering again. Cover the pan with its lid, and put it into the low moderate oven (bottom of the bottom right oven in a 4-door Aga) for 1¼ hours. Take it out, and stir in the lemon zest, nuts, tomatoes and sugar. Let it cool and keep it in the fridge until you need it.

· ·

Reheat the casserole, from room temperature, in a preheated moderate oven, 350°F/180°C/Gas Mark 4 (bottom right hand oven in a 4-door Aga), until the liquid simmers, and then let it cook, gently simmering, for at least 15 minutes. Serve.

Ham hock and bean casserole

For sheer convenience it is hard to beat this all-in-one-pot main course and it is impossible to overcook it. You can use either butter beans or cannellini beans, and vary the root vegetables if you like. You need to soak the beans the day before cooking. Have no fear about the ham hock being too salty: the potatoes take away excess saltiness. The browning of the ham hock is important, though. For those who have never bought a ham hock, it is the end of a ham: the knuckle. There's a surprising amount of meat on one. Being ham, and therefore cured, it is usually soaked before being cooked, but there really is no need for pre-soaking in this recipe. The resulting dish is intensely satisfying to eat, especially on a cold winter's day. And it is economical too. (See photograph facing page 128.)

Serves 6

3 tbsp olive oil

1 large ham hock

3 onions, *or* 6 banana shallots, skinned and finely chopped

3 leeks, trimmed, washed and sliced about ½ in/1 cm thick

3 medium potatoes, peeled and chopped into 1-in/2.5 cm chunks

3 carrots, peeled and chopped into 1-in/2.5 cm chunks

2 parsnips, peeled and chopped into 1-in/2.5 cm chunks

½ turnip, peeled and chopped into 1-in/2.5 cm chunks

1 lb/450 g dried butter beans *or* cannellini beans,
   soaked overnight in cold water then drained

1 x 15-oz/425 g can chopped tomatoes

3 pints/1.8 litres vegetable stock – use Marigold powder or Kallo cubes

3 fat cloves of garlic, skinned and chopped

plenty of freshly ground black pepper

Preheat the oven to 250°F/125°C/Gas Mark ½.

Heat the olive oil in a large casserole or saucepan, and brown the ham hock on all sides. Remove it from the pan and put in the onions and leeks. Sauté them for 5 minutes or so, then add the other vegetables and the beans. Stir in the tomatoes, stock, garlic and pepper.

Let the liquid come to the boil, replace the ham hock in the pan, bring the liquid back to a simmer and cover with a lid. Put it into the slow oven (top left oven in a 4-door Aga), for at least 4 hours. (NB The liquid in pan *must* be simmering before you put on the lid and put it into the oven. And 4 hours' cooking – or even 6 – won't be too much!) Then take it out of the oven and lift the ham hock out. The meat should fall from the bone. Discard the bone and put the meat back in with the beans and vegetables. Set aside to reheat later, or keep warm in a low oven.

· ·

Serve warm (or reheated) from the oven.

Pork ragout with tomatoes, cream and cinnamon

I use pork shoulder for this and other pork recipes that need lengthy cooking. This cut may not be expensive but it is the best for this method of cooking and the finished dish is worthy of a party. The hint of cinnamon complements the tomatoes and apple juice, and for those of you who gasp at the double cream in the list of ingredients, just look at the number of people who are going to eat this dish: six! The amount of cream per person is negligible. I like to serve this dish with well-mashed potatoes containing crispy fried leeks, and a green vegetable such as Brussels sprouts or Savoy cabbage.

Serves 6

3 tbsp flour
½ tsp salt
a good grinding of black pepper
1 tsp cinnamon
2 lb/900 g pork shoulder, trimmed and cut into 1-in-/2.5-cm chunks
3 tbsp olive oil
6 banana shallots, skinned and finely chopped
2 x 15-oz/425-g cans chopped tomatoes, whizzed smooth in a food-processor
1 pint/600 ml dry cider *or* unsweetened apple juice
½ pint/300 ml double cream

Preheat the oven to 350°C/180°C/Gas Mark 4.

Put the flour, salt, pepper and cinnamon into a polythene bag and shake well to mix. Add the pork and shake vigorously to coat it with the seasoned flour.

Heat the olive oil in a casserole or stewpan and brown the meat in small batches, turning the pieces over so that they brown on all sides. As it browns, scoop it out with a slotted spoon into a warmed dish. Then sauté the shallots over a medium heat, stirring occasionally, until they are soft and beginning to turn brown. Shake in any flour left in the polythene bag and cook for a minute, then add the puréed tomatoes and the cider or apple juice. Stir until it boils, then replace the browned meat, and stir until it boils again.

Cover the casserole with its lid, and put it into the moderate oven (bottom right oven in a 4-door Aga), for 1 hour. Lower the heat to

meat and game

slow, 250°F/125°C/Gas Mark ½ (top left oven in a 4-door Aga), and continue to cook for a further 45 minutes. Take it out of the oven, cool and store it in the fridge.

. . . .

To reheat, put the casserole on to the hob and bring it to a simmer. Pour in the cream, and bring it back to a simmer, stirring from time to time. Cook gently for 15–20 minutes, with the liquid barely bubbling, stirring occasionally. Then serve.

Ham and mushrooms *au gratin*

I love anything au gratin because it has to be prepared entirely in advance. This dish depends for its excellence on the ham. Make it, perhaps, when you have cooked a good, large ham and want an alternative to eating it cold. Ham and mushrooms are as good a combination as tomatoes and basil. Serve with baked or mashed potatoes, rice, or pasta with olive oil and parsley.

Serves 6

1 lb/450 g field mushrooms, wiped and chopped into large pieces
4 tbsp olive oil
½ tsp salt
4 banana shallots, skinned and finely sliced
1 rounded tbsp flour
1 pint/600 ml chicken stock, or ham stock, if you have it left over from cooking the ham and it isn't too salty
½ pint/300 ml double cream
1½–2 lb/675–900g cooked ham, cut into finger-thick julienne strips
3 oz/75 g Parmesan, coarsely grated
a good grinding of black pepper
a grating of nutmeg

Preheat the oven to 400°F/200°C/Gas Mark 6.

Line a baking tray with baking parchment. Put on to it the mushrooms, and, with your hands, rub in 2 tablespoons of the olive oil and the salt. Roast them in the hot oven (top right oven in a 4-door Aga) for 25–30 minutes, shuffling them about once during the cooking time. They should be almost crisp. Allow them to cool.

Meanwhile, heat the remaining olive oil in a saucepan and sauté the shallots until they are very soft, about 5 minutes. Stir in the flour and let it cook for 1 minute before gradually adding the stock, stirring all the time, until it bubbles. Stir in the cream and let it bubble for 2–3 minutes. Season with pepper and nutmeg.

Let the sauce cool before you add the cooled roast mushrooms and the ham. Pour it into an oiled ovenproof dish, cover the top with the Parmesan and store it in the fridge.

meat and game

· ·

To reheat, bake the ham and mushroom dish from room temperature in a preheated moderate oven, 350°F/180°C/Gas Mark 4 (bottom right oven in a 4-door Aga), for 20–25 minutes. Allow an extra 20 minutes' cooking time if the dish goes into the oven straight from the fridge. Finish off the gratin under the grill to brown the top, if you like. Serve.

Ham, spinach and cheese lasagne

This combines typically Florentine ingredients in a lasagne – that most useful of pasta dishes. It can be made up to 2 days in advance and kept, covered, in the fridge ready to pop into the oven. It doesn't freeze satisfactorily, though – the spinach, however carefully you cook it, tends to seep on thawing.

Serves 6

3 oz/75 g baby spinach leaves
2 tbsp olive oil
2 oz/50 g butter
2 onions, skinned and chopped
2 level tbsp flour
2 tsp Dijon mustard
½ tsp salt
a good grinding of black pepper
a grating of nutmeg
1½ pints/900 ml milk
4 oz/110 g Cheddar, grated
1½ lb/675 g cooked ham, fat removed, diced small
12 sheets lasagne
2 oz/50 g Parmesan, coarsely grated

Rub an ovenproof dish with olive oil.

Pack the spinach into a steamer or into a large sauté pan, add 2–3 tablespoons of water and cram the lid on top, then steam or cook until the leaves wilt – about 2 minutes. Heat the oil and melt the butter together in a fairly large saucepan or sauté pan, and put in the onions. Sauté them over a moderate heat until they are beginning to turn golden brown – about 5–7 minutes. Stir in the flour, and let it cook for a minute, then mix in the Dijon mustard, salt, pepper and nutmeg. Pour in the milk gradually, stirring until the sauce thickens and boils. Take the pan off the heat, and stir in the Cheddar until it has melted.

With scissors, snip the wilted spinach fairly finely, and stir it into the cheese and onion sauce. Starting and ending with a layer of cheese and onion sauce, layer the sauce, ham and lasagne sheets in the oiled dish. Scatter the grated Parmesan over the top. Store in the fridge until you need it.

· ·

To reheat the lasagne, bring it to room temperature 30 minutes before baking it in a preheated moderate oven, 350°F/180°C/Gas Mark 4 (bottom right oven in a 4-door Aga), for 35–45 minutes. (If you bake it straight from the fridge, allow another 30 minutes.)

When it is ready the sauce will be bubbling, the pasta should feel soft when you stick a knife into the centre of the lasagne, and the Parmesan will be melted and golden brown. It will then keep warm in a low oven for up to 45 minutes if you are not ready to serve it at once – any longer, and it starts to dry out.

Goulash

There are many different versions of goulash in central Europe, so I hope I will get away with mine! Sometimes it is more of a substantial soup than a stew, at others it is dry. I love them all and I'm sure I'll encounter yet more variations on the theme. You can make this one at least a day in advance, and it freezes excellently. You can serve this with noodles, but I much prefer it with very well mashed potatoes and stir-fried Savoy cabbage or steamed Brussels sprouts.

Serves 6

3 tbsp olive oil
4 onions, skinned and thinly sliced
2 lb/900 g pork shoulder, trimmed of any fat, cut into 1 in/2.5 cm chunks (buy 2½ lb/1.1 kg)
½ tsp salt
a good grinding of black pepper
1 rounded tbsp best-quality paprika
1 pint/600 ml water
1 tbsp lemon juice
½ pint/300 ml double cream

Preheat the oven to 350°/180°C/Gas Mark 4.

Heat the olive oil in a flameproof casserole and sauté the sliced onions over a moderate heat until they are very soft and starting to caramelize, turning golden brown. Scoop them out of the pan and into a warmed dish. Brown the pork, a little at a time, on all sides. Put it, too, in the warmed dish. When all of the pork has been browned, replace it with the onions in the casserole, season with salt, pepper and paprika and stir well together – don't let the paprika scorch. Pour in the water, mix well and bring the liquid to a simmer. Cover the casserole and put it into the moderate oven (bottom right oven in a 4-door Aga), for 1 hour. Allow to cool and store in the fridge.

. . . .

To reheat, take the casserole into room temperature for 30 minutes, bring it to a simmer on the hob and cook gently, lid off, for 10 minutes. Then stir in the lemon juice and cream. Bring it back to a very gentle simmer for a few more minutes, then serve.

Pheasant breasts marinated and baked

in red wine and orange

Simple to prepare and cook, and light to eat, which means you have leeway with richness – cream, cheese, etc. – in the first course and pud. Serve it with well-mashed potatoes and a green vegetable, perhaps Savoy cabbage steamed or stir-fried. Use the carcass to make stock. Be generous with the pheasant breasts; they shrink quite a bit when cooked.

Serves 6

1 pint/600 ml red wine
2 fat cloves of garlic, skinned
2 tsp salt
4 tbsp strong soy sauce – Kikkoman's or Superior Soy
8 oz/225 g jellied marmalade
4 oz/110 g butter
6–12 pheasant breasts, skin on: if they are small, i.e. from a hen pheasant,
allow 2 per person

Put all of the ingredients except the pheasant into a saucepan over a medium heat. Let the marmalade and the butter melt in the liquid, but don't let it boil. Take the pan off the heat, and leave it to cool. Put the pheasant breasts into a wide dish – don't stack them. Pour the cold marinade over them, and leave them for 24 hours, turning them once.

. . . .

Bake the pheasant in its marinade in a preheated hot oven, 400°F/200°C/Gas Mark 6 (top right oven in a 4-door Aga), for 30–35 minutes, basting from time to time. When the pheasant is done, it will keep warm in a low oven, covered, for up to 1 hour.

Venison braised with raisins and ginger

Venison is every bit as good as beef and lamb when it comes to stewing, casseroling or braising. It has such a distinctive flavour, and is so versatile. In this dish, I like to use the semi-dried raisins, which are the plumpest and juiciest to be found, better, even, than Lexia raisins, my second choice, which are available from good health-food shops and delicatessens. Once the long, slow cooking time is up, the ginger will have kept its flavour but lost its ferocity. This casserole is good with sliced potatoes baked in stock, and with steamed sugarsnap peas or, in winter months, with Brussels sprouts or Savoy cabbage. You can make it 2 days in advance.

Serves 6

2 tbsp flour

½ tsp salt

a good grinding of black pepper

2 lb/900 g venison, weighed when trimmed of gristle and membrane, cut into 1-in/2.5 cm chunks (buy about 2½ lb/1.1 kg)

3 tbsp olive oil

6 banana shallots, skinned and finely sliced

1–2 cloves of garlic, skinned and very finely chopped

3-in/7.5-cm piece root ginger, skinned and chopped

4 oz/110 g best plump, juicy raisins

1 pint/600 ml stock, either beef *or* vegetable

½ pint/300 ml red wine

Preheat the oven to 350°F/180°C/Gas Mark 4.

Put the flour, salt and pepper into a polythene bag and shake. Then put in the venison and shake vigorously, to coat each chunk with seasoned flour. Now heat the olive oil in a flameproof casserole, and brown the venison, a few chunks at a time. Remove it to a warm dish. When all the meat is browned, lower the heat under the casserole and put in the shallots. Cook them – adding another spoonful of olive oil if you think it is needed – for several minutes, until they are very soft. Then add the garlic and ginger, and continue to cook for a couple of minutes. Pour in the stock and wine, stirring all the time and scraping the bottom of the casserole to stir in any bits of

meat and game

venison and flour from the meat browning. When the liquid is simmering, replace the meat in the casserole, add the raisins, bring it back to a simmer, then cover it and put it into the moderate oven (bottom right oven in a 4-door Aga) for 1 hour. Take it out of the oven, let it cool, then store it in the fridge. You can do this 2 days in advance. (This is two-thirds of the total cooking time needed.)

. . . .

On the day of serving, bring the casserole to room temperature for 30 minutes before putting it into a preheated moderate oven, 350°F/180°C/Gas Mark 4 (bottom right oven in a 4-door Aga). Reheat until the sauce simmers – about 20 minutes – then continue to cook, simmering, for a further 25–30 minutes. It will then keep warm very satisfactorily in a low oven until you are ready to serve it.

Venison braised with root vegetables

with lemon dumplings

This is a heartening dish for a cold dreary day – really, it's the essence of comfort food. It is convenient, too: like all stews and casseroles it benefits from being made in advance and reheated – the flavours come together so much better than if it is made and eaten straight away. It freezes well, too – but the dumplings must *be cooked only in the last heating of the casserole. They take just seconds to mix, and you won't need any other starch accompaniment, unless you're feeding very hungry people, in which case baked jacket potatoes are best. A green vegetable, such as Savoy cabbage, is the perfect accompaniment.*

Serves 6

2 tbsp flour

½ tsp salt

a good grinding of black pepper

2 lb/900 g venison, weighed when trimmed of gristle, cut into 1-in/2.5-cm chunks (buy 2½ lb/1.1 kg)

4 tbsp olive oil

2 onions, skinned and finely sliced

2 leeks, trimmed, washed, and cut into 1-in/2.5-cm chunks

2 carrots, peeled and cut into 1-in/2.5-cm chunks

2 parsnips, peeled and cut into 1-in/2.5-cm chunks

½ turnip (swede), skinned and cut into 1-in/2.5-cm chunks

2 pints/1.2 litres vegetable stock

¼ pint/150 ml red wine

1 tsp redcurrant jelly

2 tsp balsamic vinegar

for the lemon dumplings

8 oz/225 g self-raising flour

8 oz/225 g suet

½ tsp salt

a good grinding of black pepper

grated zest of 2 lemons

Preheat the oven to 350°F/180°C/Gas Mark 4.

First, deal with the venison. Put the flour, salt and pepper into a polythene bag and shake it. Then add the venison and shake again to coat it with the seasoned flour. Heat the oil in a large flameproof stewpan or casserole, then brown the meat well, a little at a time, on all sides. Remove it to a warm dish with a slotted spoon. Lower the heat a little under the pan, and sauté the onions until they are just beginning to turn brown at the edges, about 5 minutes. Then stir in the leeks, carrots, parsnips and turnip and fry for a few more minutes. Replace the browned meat with the vegetables, pour in the stock and red wine, and stir until the liquid is simmering, scraping the base of the pan. Add the redcurrant jelly and the balsamic vinegar, stir, and cover with a tight-fitting lid. Put the pan into the moderate oven (bottom right oven in a 4-door Aga) for 1 hour, then reduce the heat to slow, 250°F/125°C/Gas Mark 2, and cook for a further 45 minutes (top left oven in a 4-door Aga). Take it out of the oven, let it cool completely and store it in the fridge.

To make the dumplings, put all the ingredients into a bowl and mix thoroughly. Then add just enough cold water to bind the mixture into a firm dough. Roll it into even-sized golf-balls. Cover in clingfilm and store in the fridge.

. . . .

To reheat, take the casserole into room temperature for 1 hour, then, on the hob, heat it gently until the sauce around the meat and vegetables is simmering. Put the dumplings into the casserole, pushing them down into the sauce, cover with the lid and simmer for 30 minutes.

Game and cranberry pie

This is an excellent way to use up odds and ends of game. I love cranberries, and they go so well with game and just a hint of orange. You can use virtually any game – perhaps a mixture of pheasant, hare or rabbit, old grouse or partridge, and venison. Serve it hot with a purée of root vegetables, and, perhaps, spicy red cabbage, or cold with the Stir-fried Beetroot on page 164.

Serves 6

2 rounded tbsp plain flour

2 tsp salt

a good grinding of black pepper

finely grated zest of 1 orange

2 lb/900 g raw game meat, off-the-bone weight, in 1-in/2.5-cm chunks

3 tbsp olive oil

4 banana shallots, skinned and chopped

8 oz/225 g fresh or frozen cranberries

1 pint/600 ml game *or* vegetable *or* chicken stock

½ pint/300 ml red wine

1 lb/450 g puff pastry, Saxby's or Bell's

a little milk

1 egg, beaten

Preheat the oven to 300°F/150°C/Gas Mark 3.

Put the flour, salt, pepper and orange zest into a polythene bag, add the game meat and shake vigorously until each piece is coated with seasoned flour. Heat the oil in a large ovenproof pan and brown the meat, a little at a time. Remove it with a slotted spoon to a warm dish. Lower the heat a little, and sauté the chopped shallots for about 5 minutes, or until they are soft and transparent. Replace the game in the pan, add the cranberries, and gradually stir in the stock and red wine, stirring until the liquid is simmering. Cover the pan with its lid, and put it into the low moderate oven (bottom of the bottom right oven in a 4-door Aga) for 1 hour. Take it out, let it cool, and put the game and its sauce into a pie dish. Increase the oven temperature to 400°F/200°C/Gas Mark 6.

On a floured surface, roll out the puff pastry to cover the pie, allowing an overlap of 1 in/2.5 cm all around the edge. Moisten the edge of the dish with milk then cover the pie with the pastry. With a fork, crimp this to form a corrugated ridge. Slash the top about 4 times with a sharp knife. If you like, make decorations with the leftover puff pastry – leaves are easiest – then brush the surface of the pie with the beaten egg, stick them on and brush them, too, with egg. Bake the pie for 20–30 minutes in the hot oven (top right oven in a 4-door Aga) until the pastry is deeply golden and well puffed up.

· ·

Take the pie out of the oven, and serve it hot – it will keep warm in a low oven for up to an hour – or let it cool and serve it cold.

Jugged rabbit with forcemeat balls

Hare is more usually jugged than rabbit, but for some, hare tastes too strong. Rabbit is milder, yet still more interesting than most mass-produced chicken. The drawback to using rabbit for jugging is that you never buy blood with a jointed rabbit the way it is possible to buy fresh hare with its blood. If you shoot your own rabbits, collect the blood for the purpose of jugging. If you buy rabbit and therefore don't have the blood, increase the amount of port. You can make this dish the day before you need it.

Serves 6

4 tbsp olive oil
6 x 5-oz/150 g rabbit joints
2 onions, skinned and each stuck with 6 cloves
2 carrots, peeled and roughly chopped
2 sticks of celery, chopped
2 cloves of garlic, peeled and halved
pared rind of ½ lemon
pared rind of ½ orange
1 tbsp black peppercorns
1 tsp flaky salt

for the forcemeat balls

3 tbsp olive oil
2 banana shallots, *or* 1 onion, skinned and very finely chopped
4 oz/110 g fresh white breadcrumbs
2 oz/50 g shredded suet
1 tbsp chopped parsley
finely grated zest of 1 lemon
½ tsp salt and some freshly ground black pepper

for the sauce

stock from cooking the rabbit, strained
2 oz/50 g flour
2 oz/50 g soft butter
¼ pint/150 ml rabbit blood
½ pint/300 ml port – ¾ pint/450 ml port if no blood available
2 tsp redcurrant jelly
salt and freshly ground black pepper, to taste

Preheat the oven to 300°F/150°C/Gas Mark 3.

First, cook the rabbit. Heat the olive oil in a heavy casserole and brown the pieces of rabbit all over. Remove them to a warm dish. In the same oil, sauté the onions, carrots, celery, garlic, lemon and orange rinds for 5 minutes, stirring occasionally. Then add the peppercorns and salt, replace the rabbit, and cover the contents of the pan with cold water. Bring the liquid to a simmer then cover the casserole with its lid and put it into the low moderate oven (bottom of the bottom right oven in a 4-door Aga) for 1½–2 hours, or until the meat is just beginning to pull back from the bones. Take the casserole out of the oven.

Meanwhile, make the forcemeat balls: heat the olive oil in a saucepan, and sauté the shallots,or onion, until they are soft. Then, in a bowl, mix the shallots with the breadcrumbs, suet, parsley, lemon zest and seasoning. With your hands, knead the mixture together, then roll it into walnut-sized balls and coat them with flour. Heat 2 tablespoons (or more) of olive oil in a sauté pan, and fry the forcemeat balls until they are golden brown. You can make these hours in advance, even a day ahead. Let them cool and store them in the fridge.

To make the sauce for the jugged rabbit, strain 2 pints/1.2 litres of the stock from around the rabbit joints. Put it into a large saucepan or sauté pan over a moderate heat. In a bowl work the flour into the butter until you have a paste, then stir it into the heating stock until it bubbles. Boil for 1 minute, then add the blood, the port and the redcurrant jelly, and let it boil again. Taste, and season if necessary. Cool and store in the fridge until needed.

. . . .

Reheat the forcemeat balls in a low oven for 30 minutes. Put the rabbit into the sauce, and heat it through gently – let it simmer for 10 minutes. Serve the rabbit in its sauce with the forcemeat balls handed separately.

Vegetables

and salads

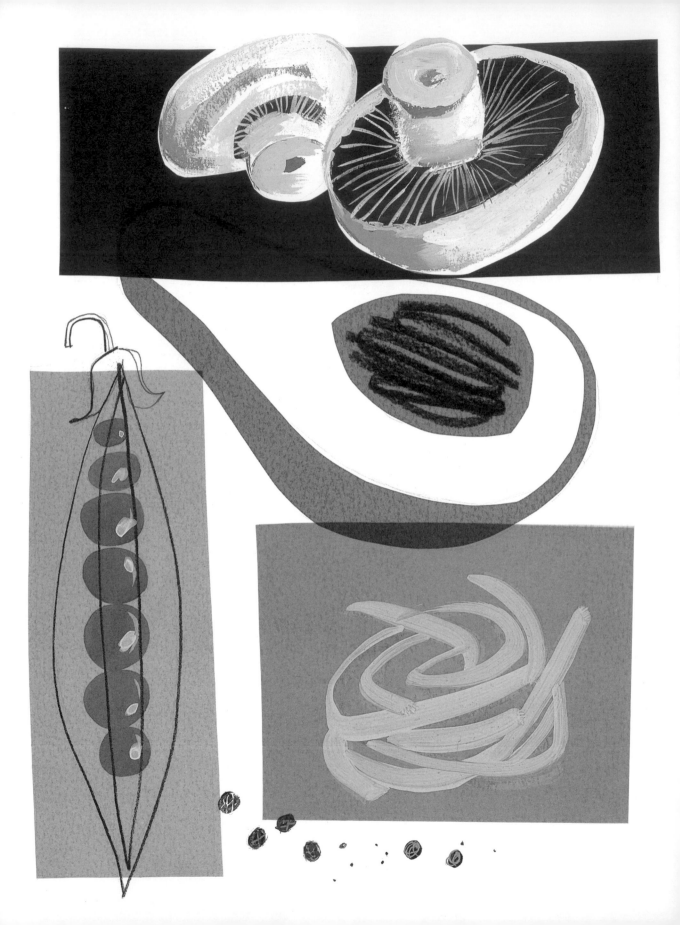

In this chapter you will find a variety of recipes to accompany a main course of meat, fish, chicken or game. Nothing needs to be cooked, drained and served at the last minute – that is the point of this book and the recipes in this chapter are no exception! In most cases all or part of the recipe can be prepared in advance. Many dishes can be served either hot or at room temperature.

Several make excellent first courses, for example, Stir-fried Beetroot with Orange, Shallots and Balsamic Vinegar on page 164, with or without the grilled goat's cheese. Other recipes make a splendid main course either for vegetarians or meat-eaters: why not try the Cheese and Tomato Pudding (page 182) for a mid-week supper and serve it with Leeks Braised with Lemon, Onions, Tomatoes and Black Olives on page 192? Or Warm Potato and Hard-boiled Egg Salad (page 186), with Marinated Cauliflower Salad (page 170), might be just the thing for Sunday evening.

Pasta is a staple in this Macdonald household, and I love it with the Spinach with Shallots, Pine Nuts and Gorgonzola mixture that you will find on page 172. I am equally fond of Vegetable Carbonara (page 168) – not to mention Spinach and Lemon Pasta (page 193), for which the sauce can be prepared entirely hours ahead. So I hope you'll find help and inspiration in this chapter to make life easier without sacrificing delicious eating.

Roast potatoes in spicy tomato sauce

This potato dish is delicious, and an interesting texture combination of crispy potatoes and smooth sauce. The piquant flavours in the sauce make it an ideal dish to serve with plain grilled, baked or barbecued meat or fish, with only a mixed leaf salad required to complete the main course. The sauce can be made a couple of days in advance. It can also be frozen.

Serves 6

for the sauce

3 tbsp olive oil

2 onions, skinned and finely sliced

1–2 cloves of garlic, skinned and finely chopped

1 x 15-oz/425-g can chopped tomatoes

¼ pint red wine

2 tsp redcurrant jelly

2 tbsp Worcester sauce

1 tsp chilli flakes

1 tbsp tomato purée

2 tsp salt

a good grinding of black pepper

2 lb/900 g new potatoes, scrubbed

olive oil

½ tsp salt

Make the sauce: heat the olive oil in a frying pan and sauté the onions until they are beginning to turn golden brown, about 5 minutes. Add the chopped garlic, cook it for a minute, then put in the tomatoes, red wine, redcurrant jelly, Worcester sauce, chilli flakes, tomato purée, salt and pepper. Bring the pan to a simmer and cook for 10 minutes, with the pan uncovered. Take it off the heat, let it cool and store it in the fridge to reheat later.

. . . .

To cook the potatoes, preheat the oven to 420°F/220°C/Gas Mark 6. Line a baking tray with baking parchment. Cut the larger potatoes in half to make them all more or less the same size. Pour enough olive oil over the potatoes to coat them, and scatter salt over them.

vegetables and salads

Put them into the hot oven (top right oven in a 4-door Aga) for 15 minutes, then turn them over, and continue to cook them until they are crisp. Take the tin out of the oven. With a slotted spoon, lift the potatoes out of the tin and put them into a warmed serving dish. Pour the reheated sauce over them.

The potatoes will keep warm satisfactorily in a low oven for 45 minutes–1 hour, loosely covered with baking parchment – not foil, which causes the potatoes to steam and lose their crispness.

Potato, cheese and bacon fritters

A tasty accompaniment to any main course or a main course in their own right. If the latter, I like to serve them with a Tomato and Chilli Sauce, see page 16. They can be made and cooked well in advance of being served – they will keep well in a low oven for over an hour.

Serves 6

2 tbsp olive oil

2 medium onions, skinned and very finely chopped

2 lb/900 g potatoes, weighed when peeled, grated

3 oz/75 g Cheddar, grated

8 rashers smoked streaky bacon, grilled till crisp then crumbled

2 tbsp chopped parsley

2 oz/50 g plain flour

½ tsp salt

a good grinding of black pepper

a grating of nutmeg

2 eggs, beaten

light olive oil for frying

Heat the 2 tablespoons of olive oil in a sauté pan, and sauté the onions for 2–3 minutes. Then, with a slotted spoon, scoop them into a bowl, with the grated potato. Add the cheese, bacon and parsley. Sieve in the flour with the salt, pepper and nutmeg and, lastly, pour in the beaten eggs. With your hands, mix everything together. Pour the light olive oil into a sauté pan to a depth of about ½ in/1 cm. Drop tablespoonsful of the potato mixture into the hot oil – cook 5–6 fritters at one time – and fry them on one side for about 5 minutes then on the other side for 4–5 minutes. As they turn crisp and deep golden brown, lift them out of the pan on to a large dish lined with a couple of thicknesses of kitchen paper to absorb excess oil.

. . . .

Keep the fritters warm in a low oven until you are ready to serve them.

Char-grilled chicken with warm noodles in a Thai dressing (page 102)

vegetables and salads

Rösti potatoes with shallots and chilli

I always think that rösti potatoes are rather lacking in taste – all you have is the texture: crisp outside and meltingly soft within. This version, however, has added taste thanks to the shallots and chilli. Don't be squeamish about the amount of butter and oil – you really do need both and in those quantities.

Serves 6

2 lb/900 g potatoes, weighed when peeled
3 banana shallots *or* 1 fairly large onion, skinned
1 level tsp dried chilli flakes
½ tsp salt
a good grinding of black pepper
3 oz/75 g butter
3 tbsp olive oil, perhaps more

Cook the potatoes in boiling salted water for 5 minutes. Drain them well, then return them in the hot dry pan to a very low heat and briefly steam them to drive off any excess moisture. Allow to cool, and when they are cool enough to handle comfortably – or several hours later when they are cold – grate them coarsely into a bowl. Then grate in the shallots or onion, and add the chilli flakes. Season with salt and pepper, and mix everything together thoroughly. Cover and set aside until you are ready to cook.

. . . .

Melt the butter and heat the oil together in a sauté pan. When it is very hot, put in the potato mixture, and press it down into the pan. Cook over a moderate heat with the pan covered for about 8 minutes. Then, slip the rösti cake on to a plate, and turn it over to cook on the other side for about 8 minutes, with the pan covered. You may need to add more olive oil to the pan before you replace the rösti. If so, heat it before you slip back the rösti.

The rösti will keep warm in a low oven for about 30 minutes, uncovered. To serve, cut it into wedges.

Pink grapefruit and avocado salad with herb and red onion vinaigrette (page 165)

Mashed potatoes with horseradish cream

Mashed potatoes are great comfort food, and go especially well with any gravy or meat sauce. They are enhanced by the addition of flavours and other ingredients that complement the main dish they will accompany. This mash, which has horseradish and cream beaten into it, is delicious with any beef, venison or pork dish. And it can be made about an hour in advance and kept warm in a low oven until you need it.

Serves 6

2 lb/900 g potatoes, weighed after peeling, and cut into similar-sized chunks
½ pint/300 ml single cream
2 tbsp best horseradish relish *or* cream
¼ pint/150 ml milk
½ tsp salt
a good grinding of black pepper
2 tbsp snipped chives, optional
a little butter

Boil the potatoes in salted water. When they are done drain them well, then return in the hot dry pan to a very low heat and briefly steam them to remove any excess moisture. Mash them very thoroughly. Then, with a wooden spoon, beat them with the cream, horseradish, milk, salt and pepper until they are fluffy. *Do not* purée them in a food-processor, which will turn them into something like wallpaper paste. Lastly, beat in the snipped chives. Butter an oven-proof dish, and pile the potatoes into it. Cover with a piece of baking parchment, and keep in a low oven until you are ready to serve.

vegetables and salads

New potatoes with cracked black pepper, pinhead oatmeal and crispy bacon

Buy new potatoes selectively: some taste of nothing, while others are so good that you'll need to double the amount suggested here. This recipe benefits from being served with a sauce – best of all a mayonnaise, if it complements the rest of the main course.   **Serves 6**

2 lb/900 g new potatoes, washed, large ones cut up to match the smaller ones
2 oz/50 g butter
3 oz/75 g pinhead oatmeal
½–1 tsp salt
2 tsp black peppercorns, bashed with a pestle in a mortar, or very coarsely ground
6 rashers smoked streaky bacon, grilled till crisp, then crumbled

Steam the potatoes until they are tender, and put them into an oven-proof dish. Meanwhile, melt the butter in a sauté pan and sauté the oatmeal, salt and black pepper, stirring occasionally, until the oatmeal is light brown. Mix in the crumbled bacon, and spoon the mixture over the new potatoes. Cover lightly, with baking parchment, and keep warm in a low oven for up to 1 hour until you are ready to serve.

Stir-fried beetroot with orange, shallots

and balsamic vinegar and grilled goat's cheese

Serves 6

Without the goat's cheese, this makes a delicious vegetable accompaniment to any meat, chicken, game or fish dish. Or you can serve it as a first course or as a simple main course with the goat's cheese. Your fingers will stain as you grate the beetroot, but the colour will wash off easily. Or you can wear rubber gloves. The beetroot mixture can be stir-fried several hours in advance, and reheated in the sauté pan before serving.

3 tbsp olive oil
4 banana shallots, skinned and sliced thinly
2 lb/900 g beetroot, weighed when peeled, coarsely grated
finely grated zest of 2 oranges
2 tsp balsamic vinegar
½ tsp salt
6 x ½-in/1-cm thick slices goat's cheese, if desired
a good grinding of black pepper

Heat the olive oil in a sauté pan and sauté the sliced shallots for about 3 minutes, stirring, until they are soft. Add the grated beetroot and the orange zest and stir, over a fairly high heat, for 5–7 minutes. Add the balsamic vinegar, season with salt and pepper, stir everything together thoroughly, and either divide it between 6 warmed plates or, if you are serving it as an accompanying vegetable, pile it into an ovenproof dish and keep it warm until you need it or set aside to reheat later.

. . . .

If the dish is to be served as a first or main course, lay the cheese on a foil-lined baking tray, and grill it for less than 1 minute – the surface should be bubbling and just turning golden. With a spatula, slip a slice on to each plate of warm or reheated beetroot. Or serve the stir-fried beetroot as an accompaniment to another dish.

Pink grapefruit and avocado salad

with herb and red onion vinaigrette

This is invaluable as a salad to accompany a fish, chicken or meat main course, or served as a lovely light first course. It looks pretty, and it can even be made several hours in advance despite the avocado: just brush it with the grapefruit juice which has seeped from the grapefruit during preparation, and cover the finished salad closely with clingfilm. (See photograph facing page 161.)

Serves 6

2 tbsp snipped chives *for the*
1 tbsp chopped flat-leaf parsley *dressing*
½ red onion, skinned and very finely chopped indeed
½ tsp salt
a good grinding of black pepper
1 tsp caster sugar
1 tsp Dijon mustard
4 tbsp olive oil
3 tsp balsamic vinegar

3 pink *or* ruby grapefruit
4 avocados, or 5 if they are small

Start by mixing together all of the dressing ingredients thoroughly. Then, with a sharp serrated knife, cut the skin and pith from the grapefruit. Then, slicing in, cut out each segment, and put them into a serving bowl. With a sharp knife, peel the avocados, then slice or chop them neatly, discarding the stones. Put the avocado among the grapefruit and spoon over the dressing. Cover with clingfilm, and leave the bowl in a cool place until you are ready to serve.

. . . .

Serve at room temperature.

Steamed broccoli with olive oil, lemon, tomato and basil dressing

Serves 6

I serve this as an accompanying vegetable, but I make it in the morning and serve it at room temperature. It looks and tastes good. Steam the broccoli until the stalks are just tender. I never undercook it. People simply don't like crunchy broccoli – or cauliflower, come to that – not at Kinloch, anyway!

6 best vine tomatoes, skinned, seeded and sliced
finely grated zest and juice of 1 lemon
½ tsp salt
a good grinding of black pepper
½ tsp caster sugar
4 tbsp olive oil
a handful of basil leaves, torn into small bits
1½ lb/675 g broccoli, weighed when trimmed, cut into even-sized florets

Put the tomatoes into a bowl. Mix together the lemon zest and juice, salt, pepper, sugar and olive oil. Cover the tomatoes with the torn basil leaves, and pour over the dressing. Leave it for several hours, or overnight, but not in the fridge. Steam the broccoli until the thickest stalk is just tender when stuck with a fork. Put the warm broccoli into a serving dish, and spoon over the marinated tomatoes in their dressing. As the broccoli cools to room temperature, it absorbs the flavours of the tomatoes, the basil, and the lemony dressing.

. . . .

Serve at room temperature.

vegetables and salads

Steamed broccoli baked with butter, parsley breadcrumbs and capers

You can use cauliflower instead of broccoli, or a combination of both, which looks attractive. Although the broccoli (or cauliflower) should be steamed reasonably soon before it is served, the butter and crumb mixture can be made the day before. Use capers preserved in olive oil, not in brine or salted.

Serves 6

4 oz/110 g fresh white *or* brown bread
2 handfuls flat-leaf parsley
4 oz/110 g butter
½ tsp salt
a good grinding of black pepper
2 tsp oil-preserved capers, drained of their oil
1½ lb/675 g broccoli, cut into even-sized florets

Whiz the bread with the parsley in a food-processor until you have green-flecked crumbs. Melt the butter in a sauté pan, put in the parsley breadcrumbs and season with the salt and pepper. Fry, stirring, until the crumbs are golden brown. Then stir in the capers, and cook for a further 30 seconds or so. Set aside until needed.

. . . .

Steam the broccoli until the thickest stalk is just tender, then put it into an ovenproof dish. If you made the crumb mixture in advance, reheat it in the sauté pan before spooning it over the steamed broccoli. Scatter the crumbs over the broccoli and keep it warm in a low oven until you are ready to serve it – up to 15–20 minutes.

Vegetable carbonara

This is a pasta au gratin. Its carbonara-style sauce contains several vegetables as well as the pasta and it is both convenient – the whole thing can be made a day in advance – and delicious. Vary the vegetables according to what is in season and what you like. Add as much or as little garlic as you fancy. But the imperative is freshly grated Parmesan. Serve, if you like, with a mixed leaf salad.

Serves 6

3 tbsp olive oil

3 banana shallots, skinned and sliced

6 rashers smoked, *or* unsmoked, back bacon

8 oz/225 g mushrooms, wiped and sliced *or* chopped

6 oz/175 g shelled peas

6 oz/175 g matchstick-sliced courgettes

6 oz/175 g green beans

2 cloves of garlic, skinned and chopped finely

a few fresh thyme leaves *or* ¼ tsp dried thyme

¼ pint/150 ml white wine

½ pint/300 ml double cream

½ tsp salt

a good grinding of black pepper

a grating of nutmeg

8 oz/225 g penne, *or* other short-cut pasta

2 large egg yolks

5 oz/75 g freshly grated Parmesan

Heat the olive oil in a sauté pan, and add the shallots. With scissors – easiest – snip the fat off the bacon, then snip the meat into fine strips and put them into the pan with the shallots. Continue to cook for about 5 minutes over a fairly high heat, stirring occasionally. When the shallots are soft and turning golden brown and the bacon is done, scoop them out of the pan, with a slotted spoon, into a warmed dish, leaving as much oil behind as you can. Add the other vegetables, the garlic and thyme to the pan and cook, stirring, for 3–5 minutes. Pour in the wine and let it simmer until it has almost

vegetables and salads

evaporated. Stir in the cream and bubble for a couple of minutes. Put the bacon and shallots back into the pan, season with salt, pepper and nutmeg, and stir thoroughly.

Meanwhile, bring a saucepan of water to the boil and, when it is boiling fast, put in the pasta. Cook for 7 minutes, then drain well and mix it into the sauté pan with the vegetables.

Oil an ovenproof dish. Mix together the egg yolks with 3 oz/75 g of the Parmesan, and stir it into the pan. Tip the contents of the pan into the oiled dish and cover the surface with the remaining Parmesan. Leave it in a larder or fridge, covered, until you need it.

. . . .

Bring the carbonara back to room temperature (from a fridge it needs about 30 minutes) before baking in a preheated moderate oven, 350°F/180°C/Gas Mark 4 (bottom right oven in a 4-door Aga), until the Parmesan becomes a golden crisp crust – allow 25–30 minutes.

Marinated cauliflower salad

If you aren't keen on garlic, reduce the amount or leave it out. While cauliflower tastes good, it can look anaemic: in this recipe the herbs in the marinade 'lift' the appearance of the salad. It goes well with all meat, fish, chicken or game. You can make this in the morning to eat that evening.

Serves 6

2 small *or* 1 large cauliflower, leaves and tough stalk discarded, divided into florets
6 tbsp olive oil
3 cloves of garlic, skinned and very finely chopped *or* crushed
½ tsp salt
a good grinding of black pepper
finely grated zest and juice of 1 lemon
½ tsp caster sugar
1 tsp Dijon mustard
2 tbsp snipped chives
2 tbsp chopped flat-leaf parsley

Steam the cauliflower until it is just tender. Beware undercooking it – uncooked cauliflower tastes vile. Put it into a serving dish. While it steams, mix together the rest of the ingredients thoroughly. Spoon the dressing over the hot cauliflower in the serving dish. As it cools, it will absorb the flavours of the dressing.

Brussels sprouts with Dijon mustard

and crème fraiche

I first ate this unlikely sounding combination in a restaurant in Rome – cold, as part of a table of antipasti. I have made it ever since during the winter, to serve hot, or as a cooled cooked salad. If you are dubious, I urge you to try it and taste for yourself how good it is.

Serves 6

**2 lb/900 g Brussels sprouts, trimmed and stabbed in the base
with the point of a sharp knife
2 rounded tbsp best Dijon mustard
½ pint/300 ml full-fat crème fraiche**

Steam the sprouts until they are just tender when stuck with a fork. Don't be tempted to undercook them – they will taste revolting.

While the sprouts steam, mix together the Dijon mustard and crème fraiche. When the sprouts are cooked, stir them into the Dijon cream. Then put them into an ovenproof dish and keep them warm until you are ready to serve them. Alternatively, serve them cooled.

Spinach with shallots, pine nuts and Gorgonzola

A sumptuous accompanying vegetable to any plain main course that needs dressing up. It is particularly good with venison or beef steak. You can also use it as the main part of a pasta dish. Allow 2 oz/50 g short-cut pasta per person, boil it until al dente, drain it, then mix it into the creamily delicious spinach, pine nut and Gorgonzola mixture. Dip a knife into hot water to cut up the Gorgonzola – it makes life so much easier.

Serves 6

3 tbsp olive oil
3 oz/75 g pine nuts
6 banana shallots, skinned and thinly sliced
8 oz/225 g baby spinach leaves, steamed till just wilted
8 oz/225 g Gorgonzola, cut into small chunks

Heat the olive oil in a sauté pan, add the pine nuts and sauté them, shaking the pan, until they are deeply golden brown. Scoop them out on to kitchen paper. Put the shallots into the pan and sauté, stirring occasionally, for about 5 minutes until they are soft. Add the wilted spinach, and cook, mixing the shallots thoroughly into the spinach, for about 2 minutes. Stir in the Gorgonzola with the fried pine nuts, cook for a further minute or two, then tip the contents of the pan into a warmed ovenproof dish.

. . . .

Keep this scrummy mixture warm in a low oven until you are ready to serve.

vegetables and salads

Braised chicory with orange

We have access to the most wonderful food in the world here in Skye, but whenever I want chicory, I have to get it from Edinburgh or Glasgow. I love chicory, cooked or uncooked. In this simple recipe the chicory is slow-cooked with orange. It is sharp and astringent, a fabulous foil for fish, chicken and pork. Serve it either hot or at room temperature.

Serves 6

2 tbsp olive oil
2 banana shallots, skinned and thinly sliced
5 heads chicory, trimmed and cut into 2-in/5-cm lengths
½ pint/300 ml chicken *or* vegetable stock
finely grated zest and juice of 2 oranges
½ tsp salt
a good grinding of black pepper

Heat the olive oil in a sauté pan with a lid, and sauté the shallots for about 5 minutes until they are soft. Put in the chicory, and stir it around among the shallots for about 1 minute. Add the stock, orange juice and zest, salt and pepper. Bring it to a simmer, cover the pan with its lid, and cook for 30–35 minutes.

This will keep warm in a low oven for over an hour.

Puréed peas with shallots and mint

An excellent accompaniment to meat, chicken or fish, although it is not so good with game, or use it as a sauce-cum-garnish for grilled, baked or roast fish – serve the fish sitting on top of the purée. It looks so pretty and tastes so good however you use it. Use applemint if at all possible, but if you can't find it any other variety will do. There is no doubt about it, freshly podded peas taste much better than frozen, but I still use and love frozen peas, out of pea season.

Serves 6

2 tbsp olive oil
4 banana shallots, skinned and finely chopped
2 lb/900 g peas, weighed when shelled
½ pint/300 ml chicken stock
½ tsp salt
a good grinding of black pepper
a handful of applemint leaves
¼ pint/150 ml double cream

Heat the oil in a sauté pan and sauté the chopped shallots until they are soft – about 5 minutes. Add the peas, and stir them around among the shallots for a couple of minutes. Pour in the stock and bring it to a simmer. Cover the pan and cook for 5 minutes until the peas are soft. Take it off the heat, season with salt and pepper, and put the contents of the pan into a food-processor. Whiz until very smooth, adding the mint as you do so. Then whiz in the cream. If your food-processor blades are sharp, you should get a smooth purée, fragrant with mint. If your blades are not as sharp as they might be, you might want to sieve the purée. Have ready an oiled ovenproof dish, and scrape the pea purée into it. Cover it with baking parchment, and keep it warm in a low oven for up to 30 minutes.

Nutmeg and ginger puréed parsnips

with bacon bits

This velvety smooth purée is spiked with ginger and nutmeg, and goes well with virtually any main course, whether plain grilled or roast, stewed or casseroled. It can be made in the morning and reheated gently in a low oven for a couple of hours before serving. The bacon can be grilled and broken into bits a couple of days in advance.

Serves 6

2 lb/900 g parsnips, weighed when peeled and trimmed, cut into chunks
2-in/5-cm piece root ginger, skinned, and grated *or* finely chopped
2 oz/50 g butter, cut into 4
6 gratings of nutmeg
½ tsp salt
a good grinding of black pepper
6 rashers smoked streaky bacon, grilled until crisp, then broken into bits

Either cook the parsnips and ginger in boiling salted water or, better, steam them until the biggest chunk of parsnip is soft. If you have boiled them, drain them, and return them in the hot dry pan to a very low heat and briefly steam them to drive off excess water: about 5 seconds. Put the cooked parsnips and ginger into a food-processor and whiz to a purée. Add the butter, a piece at a time. Season with nutmeg, salt and pepper. Scrape the purée into a buttered ovenproof dish. Scatter over the bacon bits and loosely cover the dish with baking parchment.

Keep it warm in a low oven for up to 2 hours.

Spiced baked carrots

Serves 6

An excellent way to spark up carrots, and equally good hot or cooled. You can cook them a day in advance, but they are so quick and easy to prepare it hardly seems worth it.

1 tsp cumin seeds
1 tsp black peppercorns
4 tbsp olive oil
2 medium onions *or* 4 banana shallots, peeled and sliced
2 lb/900 g carrots, weighed when peeled and trimmed, cut into finger-size strips
2 cloves of garlic, skinned and sliced
½ pint/300 ml chicken *or* vegetable stock
1 tsp Tabasco
1 tbsp white wine vinegar
½ tsp salt
1 tbsp flat-leaf parsley, chopped
snipped chives

Grind together the cumin and black pepper in a mortar with a pestle. Heat the oil in an ovenproof sauté pan and sauté the onions or shallots for 3–5 minutes, then add the carrots. Stir them around for a minute, then put in the garlic, stock, Tabasco, vinegar, cumin and pepper mixture and the salt. Bring the liquid to a simmer, cover the pan, and bake in a preheated moderate oven, 350°F/180°C/Gas Mark 4 (bottom right oven in a 4-door Aga), for 15–20 minutes or until the carrots are very tender.

. . . .

Just before serving, stir in the parsley and chives – carefully, so you don't break up the softened carrot sticks.

vegetables and salads

Broad beans in crème fraiche with mustard

This dish is especially good with pork or ham – or even with grilled pork sausages and baked jacket potatoes. It can be served hot or at room temperature. It also makes an unusual – and very good – cooked salad. Mix together the crème fraiche, mustard, Demerara sugar and salt and pepper the previous day, if you like.

Serves 6

½ pint/300 ml full-fat crème fraiche
1 tbsp best Dijon mustard
1 level tbsp Demerara sugar
½ tsp salt
a grinding of of black pepper
1½ lb/675 g broad beans, weighed when shelled

Mix together the crème fraiche, mustard, Demerara sugar, salt and pepper. Steam the broad beans until tender, then stir them into the crème fraiche mixture. Put the beans in their sauce into a warmed ovenproof dish, cover with a lid if the dish has one, or if not with baking parchment.

Keep it warm in a low oven until you are ready to serve – up to 30 minutes. The sauce around the beans is fairly runny, but don't worry. It is meant to be so.

Stir-fried Savoy cabbage with nutmeg and pepper

in crème fraiche

This is particularly good with pork and game dishes. I do love Savoy cabbage, and although it doesn't keep for long after cooking without the flavour spoiling, you can prepare it in advance. The cabbage can be shredded and the shallots sautéd until soft. The actual cooking takes just minutes.

Serves 6

2 tbsp olive oil

2 oz/50 g butter

4 banana shallots, skinned and finely sliced

6 gratings of nutmeg

½ tsp salt

a very good grinding of black pepper

1 x 1½ lb/675 g Savoy cabbage, outer leaves removed and shredded

4 tbsp full-fat crème fraiche

Heat the olive oil and melt the butter in a sauté pan, and sauté the shallots until they are soft, about 5 minutes. Add the nutmeg, salt and pepper, then the cabbage. Continue to cook, stirring from time to time, until the thickest shred of cabbage is soft. Put in the crème fraiche, and stir until it melts around the cabbage.

Keep the pan covered and warm for an hour or two until you are ready to serve.

Savoy cabbage salad

with mustard seeds and crème fraiche

*Now, for this salad you can either finely shred the Savoy cabbage and leave
it raw, or you can shred it and steam if for 2 minutes, which is what I do. I
much prefer cabbage lightly steamed to raw, but you do lose a bit in texture.
On the other hand, there is plenty of texture in this salad with the apples and
celery, so do what appeals to you! It goes particularly well with hot or cold
ham or pork.*

Serves 6

2 good eating apples, *not* Golden Delicious, peeled or not, quartered, cored and chopped

2 tbsp lemon juice

1 Savoy cabbage, outer leaves and tough stalk discarded, shredded

2 tsp mustard seeds

3 sticks celery, washed, trimmed and sliced ¼ in/0.5 cm thick

½ pint/300 ml full-fat crème fraiche

2 tbsp snipped chives

½ tsp salt

a good grinding of black pepper

Put the chopped apples into a salad bowl and toss them with the
lemon juice.

Either steam the shredded cabbage for 2 minutes, or put it straight
into a serving bowl. Dry-fry the mustard seeds for 3–4 minutes, then
put them into the bowl with the cabbage. Add the celery, then mix
in the crème fraiche, chives, salt and pepper, and mix thoroughly.
Wipe any smears of crème fraiche from the sides of the bowl,
loosely cover it, and leave it in a cool place for several hours, until you
are ready to serve it.

Baked creamy onions

with butter-fried parsley breadcrumbs

This is the best vegetable dish of all to serve with lamb, especially when it is roasted or grilled, and with roast pork. It can be made in the morning for supper that evening. You can even make it a day in advance, but in that case don't put the parsley crumbs over the onions in their sauce until just before you reheat the dish for serving. Pop it into the oven to heat through shortly before you want to eat it.

Serves 6

12 onions – this sounds a lot, but they wilt down as they cook – skinned and quartered
2 pints/1.2 litres stock, *either* chicken *or* vegetable
2 oz/50 g butter, plus a little extra for greasing
3 oz/75 g white *or* brown breadcrumbs
about ¼ tsp salt
1 tbsp chopped flat-leaf parsley
2 tbsp olive oil
1 rounded tbsp flour
¼ pint/150 ml double cream
½ tsp salt
a good grinding of black pepper
a grating of nutmeg

Put the onions into a wide sauté pan with a lid, and add the stock. Bring it to a simmer, cover the pan, and cook gently until the onions are soft, about 25 minutes.

Meanwhile, butter an ovenproof dish thoroughly. Melt the 2 oz/ 50 g butter in a sauté pan and sauté the breadcrumbs with the salt, stirring, till they are evenly golden brown. Stir in the chopped parsley and fry for another minute. Take the pan off the heat, and scoop the buttery crumbs on to a warm dish lined with kitchen paper.

Measure off 1 pint/600 ml of the stock in which the onions have cooked.

Heat the olive oil in a saucepan, stir in the flour and cook for a minute. Then gradually pour in the onion stock, stirring all the time until the sauce boils. Stir in the cream, and bring the sauce back to a simmer. Season with salt, pepper and nutmeg. With a slotted spoon, lift the onions from the pan into the sauce, and stir them in well. Pour the onions and the sauce into the buttered dish, and cover the surface with the parsley crumbs. (If you are making the dish a day ahead, set the parsley crumbs aside for now. If you are making the dish on the morning of serving, you can add the parsley crumbs at this point if you like. Whichever you choose, don't forget them!) Leave in a cool place until you are ready to cook it.

· ·

To reheat the parsley-crumbed dish, put the dish – from room temperature – into a preheated moderate oven, 350°F/180°C/Gas Mark 4 (bottom right oven in a 4-door Aga), for 25 minutes or until the sauce is sizzling around the edges. Keep the dish warm in a low oven until you are ready to serve it.

Cheese and tomato pudding

Serves 6

This is a most sustaining and comforting main course. It is easy and can be prepared hours in advance, but it should be eaten soon after it is cooked – it will keep warm for an hour in a low oven, but is not nearly as good if it is reheated. Make breadcrumbs from a proper baked loaf – not a steamed one.

6 oz/175 g fresh white *or* brown bread

2 handfuls parsley

12 oz/350 g Cheddar cheese, grated – or, even better, Lancashire,
   which is excellent for cooking

2 tbsp olive oil

2 onions, skinned and very finely chopped

2 tsp Dijon *or* English mustard

½ tsp salt

a good grinding of black pepper

4 large eggs

¾ pint/450 ml milk

1 tbsp Worcester sauce

3–4 tomatoes, washed and sliced

2 oz/50 g butter, diced

Thoroughly butter a 3-pint/1.8-litre ovenproof dish.

Whiz the bread in a food-processor with the parsley until you have parsley crumbs, then mix them with three-quarters of the cheese and put them into the buttered dish. Heat the olive oil in a frying pan and sauté the the onions until they are soft. In a bowl, beat the mustard, salt and pepper with the eggs, and stir in the milk. Add the Worcester sauce, and the sautéd onions, then pour the mixture over the crumbs and cheese. Cover with the sliced tomatoes and dot with the butter. Sprinkle over the rest of the cheese. Set aside.

. . . .

When ready to cook the dish, bake it, from room temperature, in a preheated low moderate oven, 300°F/150°C/Gas Mark 2 (bottom of the bottom right oven in a 4-door Aga), for 50–60 minutes, or until the pudding is firm and set. Keep the pudding warm in a low oven.

vegetables and salads

Sweet and sour green beans

A simple way to make green beans a little more exciting. They are very good with the Cheese and Tomato Pudding opposite, or with any ham or pork dish.

Serves 6

1 tbsp olive oil
1 onion, skinned and finely chopped
1 oz/25 g flour
1 tbsp soft brown – light or dark– sugar
½ pint/300 ml vegetable *or* chicken stock
1 tbsp balsamic vinegar
1 tbsp tomato purée
½ tsp salt
1½ lb/675 g sliced *or* fine green beans, steamed until just tender
6 rashers smoked streaky bacon, grilled until crisp

Heat the olive oil in a sauté pan and sauté the onion until it is soft and beginning to turn golden brown. Stir in the flour and sugar, and cook for a minute, then add the stock, vinegar and tomato purée. Stir until the sauce bubbles, then add the salt and stir in the steamed beans.

Rub an ovenproof dish well with olive oil. Pour the beans with their sauce into it. Break up the bacon and scatter it over the top. Store in a cool place.

. . . .

Reheat from room temperature in a preheated moderate oven, 350°F/180°C/Gas Mark 4 (bottom right oven in a 4-door Aga), for 15 minutes.

Baked roast aubergines *au gratin*

Useful as a first course, or as a main course with a mixed-leaf salad and warm bread. It can be made a day in advance, and reheated before serving. The quantities given below are for a main course. It sounds as though the aubergines are twice cooked from the recipe title – and they are. By roasting the sliced aubergines you use far less oil than if you sauté the slices.

Serves 6

3 fairly large aubergines, 4 if they are small, cut into slices ½ in/1 cm thick
   (beware of the prickly stalk end)
olive oil

for the
tomato sauce

3 tbsp olive oil
2 onions, skinned and finely chopped
2 sticks celery, washed, trimmed and finely sliced
1–2 cloves of garlic, to taste, skinned and very finely chopped
2 x 15-oz/425-g cans chopped tomatoes
½ tsp salt
½ tsp caster sugar
a good grinding of pepper
2 tsp pesto

for the
cheese sauce

2 oz/50 g butter
2 oz/50 g flour
1¼ pints/750 ml milk
2 tsp Dijon or English mustard
½ tsp salt
a good grinding of black pepper
a grating of nutmeg
5 oz/150 g freshly grated Parmesan

Preheat the oven to 400°F/200°C/Gas Mark 6.

To make the tomato sauce, heat 2 tablespoons of the olive oil in a frying pan and sauté the onion and celery for about 5 minutes, until the onion is soft. Then add the garlic, tomatoes, seasonings and pesto. Let it simmer, the pan uncovered, for about 15 minutes.

Line 1 or 2 baking trays with baking parchment, brush the aubergine slices with olive oil on both sides and lay them on the tray(s). Roast them in the hot oven (top right oven in a 4-door Aga) for 15 minutes, then turn the slices and roast on the other side for a further 10–15 minutes. Take the baking tray(s) out of the oven.

Rub a large shallow ovenproof dish with olive oil. Put in some of the roast aubergine slices and spoon over some tomato sauce. Continue to layer them until both are finished.

Make the cheese sauce: melt the butter in a saucepan and stir in the flour. Let this cook for a minute, then gradually add the milk, stirring all the time until the sauce bubbles. Take the pan off the heat, and stir in the mustard, salt, pepper and nutmeg and 3 oz/75 g of the Parmesan. Pour the sauce over the aubergines, and cover the surface with the remaining Parmesan. Store in a cool place.

· ·

To reheat the dish, bring it to room temperature and bake it in a pre-heated moderate oven, 350°F/180°C/Gas Mark 4 (bottom right oven in a 4-door Aga), for 25–30 minutes. If the sauces are bubbling gently but the top is not a crisp crust of molten Parmesan, put the dish under a red-hot grill for 30 seconds. Keep it warm in a low oven until it is needed.

Warm potato and hard-boiled egg salad

I so love potatoes, hard-boiled eggs (can't stand eggs other than hard-boiled) and home-made mayonnaise. This warm salad of all three ingredients constitutes, for me, a perfect main course, especially when accompanied by a good tomato salad, and some mixed salad leaves. Home-made mayonnaise is so much better than the commercial variety, and so easy to make. You can, of course, make it a day in advance.

Serves 6

1½ lb/675 g new potatoes, either Charlotte, or Duke of York, cut, if necessary, to an even size
2 tbsp olive oil
2 tbsp snipped chives
½ tsp salt
a good grinding of black pepper
1 tsp balsamic vinegar
6 large eggs, hard-boiled, shelled and chopped
6 tbsp of the home-made mayonnaise

for the mayonnaise

2 large egg yolks
2 tsp Dijon mustard
1 tsp caster sugar
½ tsp salt
a good grinding of black pepper
½ pint/300 ml olive oil
2 tbsp white *or* red wine vinegar

To make the mayonnaise, put the yolks, mustard, sugar, salt and pepper into a food-processor and whiz, adding the olive oil drop by drop then in a steady trickle. Lastly, whiz in the vinegar. Set aside.

. . . .

Steam the potatoes until they are tender, and put them into a serving bowl or dish. Immediately stir into them the olive oil, chives, salt, pepper and balsamic vinegar. Then mix in the hard-boiled eggs and the mayonnaise. Serve the salad warm.

Baked stuffed field mushrooms

These wide flat mushrooms have so much more taste than the wretched little button mushrooms, and they are perfect *for stuffing. Stuffed mushrooms make a marvellous accompaniment to steaks, chops, grilled chicken or fish, and are ideal,too, for those who don't include meat in their diet. They also make a tasty first course. I allow 2 per person as an accompanying vegetable. You can prepare the mushrooms for baking a day in advance.*

Serves 6

4 tbsp olive oil, plus a little extra
4 red onions, skinned and very finely chopped
1–2 cloves of garlic, skinned and very finely chopped
3 tbsp chopped flat-leaf parsley
2 oz/50 g fresh white *or* brown breadcrumbs
3 oz/75 g Parmesan, coarsely grated
a good grinding of black pepper
12 flat field mushrooms, stalks trimmed but not pulled out

Heat the olive oil in a sauté pan, put in the onions and sauté until they are very soft, about 5 minutes. Then scoop them into a bowl with the garlic (if you want a less pronounced garlic taste, you could sauté the garlic with the onions) parsley, breadcrumbs, Parmesan. and pepper – no need for salt because the Parmesan is salty enough for most palates. Mix thoroughly. Put the mushrooms on an oiled baking tray, divide the stuffing between them and drizzle a little olive oil over each one. Cover them with clingfilm and leave them in a cool place until you are ready to roast them.

. . . .

Put the mushrooms into a preheated hot oven, 400°F/200°C/Gas Mark 6 (top right oven in a 4-door Aga) for 20 minutes, then check them – they will probably need another 10 minutes: they should be golden and crisp on top.

They will keep warm in a low oven for up to 1 hour, or you can serve them at room temperature.

Mushrooms, roast then baked

with shallots, cream and soy sauce

Serves 6

Another widely useful dish: serve it as an accompanying vegetable or as a first course. It's especially good with the Cheese and Tomato Pudding on page 182. It can be made in advance and reheated before serving.

1½ lb/675 g mushrooms, wiped and sliced *or* chopped
6 tbsp olive oil
½ tsp salt
4 banana shallots, skinned and sliced
½ pint/300 ml double cream
2 tbsp dark soy sauce (not light)
a good grinding of black pepper
3 oz/75 g pine nuts, dry-fried until biscuit-coloured

Preheat the oven to 400°F/200°C/Gas Mark 6.

Line a baking tray with a sheet of baking parchment. Lay on it the mushrooms and, with your hands, mix in 4 tablespoons of the olive oil. Scatter with salt, and roast in the hot oven (top right oven in a 4-door Aga) for 20 minutes. Then shuffle the mushrooms around and roast for a further 20 minutes. Take the tray out of the oven.

Meanwhile, heat the remainder of the olive oil in a sauté pan and sauté the sliced shallots until they are soft. Tip the mushrooms into the pan, stir in the cream and the soy sauce, and let the cream bubble until the sauce is as thick as you want it – the consistency of custard is what I aim for. Season with pepper.

Oil an ovenproof dish thoroughly, and pour the contents of the pan into it. Scatter over the pine nuts. Set aside in a cool place.

. . . .

Reheat the dish in a preheated moderate oven, 350°F/180°C/Gas Mark 4 (bottom right oven in a 4-door Aga), for 20 minutes from room temperature. Keep it warm in a low oven until you are ready to eat it – up to 45 minutes.

Baked spinach and mushrooms

This goes well with any meat, fish, chicken or game dish, or you could serve it as a delicious main course for vegetarians. It can be made a day in advance. **Serves 6**

1 lb/450 g mushrooms, wiped and chopped
4 tbsp olive oil, plus a little extra
2 oz/50 g fresh white *or* brown breadcrumbs
2 oz/50 g butter and ¼ tsp salt
2 medium onions, skinned and finely sliced
8 oz/225 g baby spinach leaves, steamed till just wilted
8 oz/225 g cream cheese, e.g. Philadelphia
1 tsp Tabasco
2 large eggs
½ tsp salt, a good grinding of black pepper and a grating of nutmeg

Preheat the oven to 400°F/200°C/Gas Mark 6.

Line a roasting tin with baking parchment. Lay on it the sliced mushrooms, and, with your hands, mix in 2 tablespoons of the olive oil. Roast the mushrooms in the hot oven (top right oven in a 4-door Aga) for 20 minutes, then shuffle them around, and roast for a further 10 minutes. Meanwhile, fry the breadcrumbs in the butter with the salt until they are crisp.

Heat the other 2 tablespoons of olive oil in a sauté pan and sauté the onions for about 5 minutes, or until they are beginning to turn golden brown. Add the spinach to the pan, and mix it thoroughly with the onions.

Oil an ovenproof dish and put the onions, spinach and roast mushrooms into it. Put the cream cheese into a food-processor and whiz, adding the Tabasco, eggs, salt, pepper and nutmeg as you go. Spoon this over the mushroom mixture, cover with the butter-fried crumbs and store in the fridge, covered.

. . . .

Before serving, bake the dish from room temperature in a preheated moderate oven, 350°F/180°C/Gas Mark 4 (bottom right oven in a 4-door Aga), for 25–30 minutes, until the cream cheese is firm. Keep warm in a low oven for up to 30 minutes before serving.

Mushroom and spring onion pasta *au gratin*

Serves 6

This dish has a thick layer of pasta, spinach and passata topped with a layer of creamy roast mushrooms in nutmeg-flavoured sauce with fried spring onions. As with any pasta au gratin, *you can make this a day in advance and keep it in the fridge until you need it.*

1½ lb/675 g mushrooms, wiped and sliced
5 tbsp olive oil, plus a little extra
½ tsp salt
12 oz/350 g fusilli *or* other short pasta
2 cloves of garlic, skinned and finely chopped
3 oz/75 g baby spinach leaves, steamed then finely chopped
½ pint/300 ml passata, *or* 1 x 15-oz/425-g can chopped tomatoes, puréed in a blender
2 oz/50 g butter
24 spring onions, trimmed and cut diagonally into 1-in/2.5-cm lengths
1 rounded tbsp plain flour
1¼ pints/750 ml milk
a good grinding of black pepper
a grating of nutmeg
4 oz/75 g freshly grated Parmesan

Preheat the oven to 400°F/200°C/Gas Mark 6.

Line a baking tray with baking parchment, put on it the mushrooms and, with your fingers, rub 3 tablespoons of the olive oil thoroughly into them. Sprinkle over the salt and roast in the hot oven (top right oven in a 4-door Aga) for 20 minutes. Shuffle them around on the baking tray, roast for a further 15 minutes and take them out of the oven.

Meanwhile, in a large pan of boiling salted water, cook the pasta for 7 minutes and drain well. Toss it in the remaining olive oil with the garlic, spinach and passata. Rub an ovenproof dish with olive oil and tip the pasta into it. Put the roast sliced mushrooms over the top.

In a saucepan or sauté pan melt the butter and sauté the spring onions for 3–5 minutes – they should feel fairly soft when stuck with a fork. Stir in the flour and let it cook for a minute, then pour in the milk gradually, stirring until the sauce bubbles. Take the pan off the heat, season with pepper and nutmeg, and stir in 3 oz/75 g of the Parmesan. Pour the sauce over the mushrooms, and scatter over the remaining Parmesan.

Leave it to cool and store it in the fridge.

. . . .

To reheat the dish, let it come to room temperature first (it needs about 30 minutes), then put it into a preheated moderate oven, 350°F/180°C/Gas Mark 4 (bottom right oven in a 4-door Aga), for 30 minutes, until the top is golden and crisp.

Leeks braised with lemon, onions,

tomatoes and olives

Another vegetable dish that will accompany any grilled meat, chicken or fish. It is also very good served at room temperature as a first course. It can be prepared in advance and then reheated if you want to serve it hot.

Serves 6

10 medium leeks, trimmed and washed
3 tbsp olive oil
2 medium onions, skinned and finely chopped
finely grated zest and juice of 1 lemon
about 12 best black olives, stoned and chopped
½ pint/300 ml chicken stock
½ tsp salt
a good grinding of black pepper
3 vine tomatoes, skinned, seeded and sliced

Cut the leeks on the diagonal into slices about 1 in/2.5 cm thick. Heat the olive oil in a sauté pan, and sauté the onions for about 5 minutes, or until they are soft and just beginning to turn golden at the edges. Then add the leeks and cook for a couple of minutes. Add the lemon juice and zest, the olives and the stock. Season with salt and pepper, bring the liquid to a gentle simmer, cover the pan with a lid and cook gently for 12–15 minutes. Then take the pan off the heat, and add the tomatoes.

. . . .

Keep the leeks warm in a low oven for an hour or more or let them cool and serve at room temperature in a pretty dish – white is best.

Leeks braised with lemons, onions, tomatoes and olives

vegetables and salads

Spinach and lemon pasta

This recipe is quick and delicious – like a carbonara but with lemon and Parmesan instead of bacon. The eggs and cream can be beaten together, and the spinach wilted, hours in advance. It takes about 10 minutes to cook the pasta, and you don't need anything else to accompany it.

Serves 6

1 large egg
2 egg yolks
finely grated zest of 2 lemons
½ pint/300 ml full-fat creme fraiche
1–2 cloves of garlic, to taste, skinned and very finely chopped
8 oz/225 g baby spinach leaves, steamed till just wilted, then chopped – I use scissors
½ tsp salt
a good grinding of black pepper
12 oz/350 g spaghetti
1 tbsp olive oil
freshly grated Parmesan cheese, to hand separately

Beat together the egg, yolks, lemon zest, crème fraiche and garlic, then stir in the spinach. Season with salt and pepper.

. . . .

Bring a large saucepan of salted water to the boil, put in the spaghetti and boil for about 6 minutes. Test, with your thumbnail, to see if it is cooked *al dente*, then drain. Stir in the olive oil, then fork the spinach and lemon cream thoroughly through the hot pasta. Serve immediately, and pass round the Parmesan.

Spinach and lemon pasta

Puddings

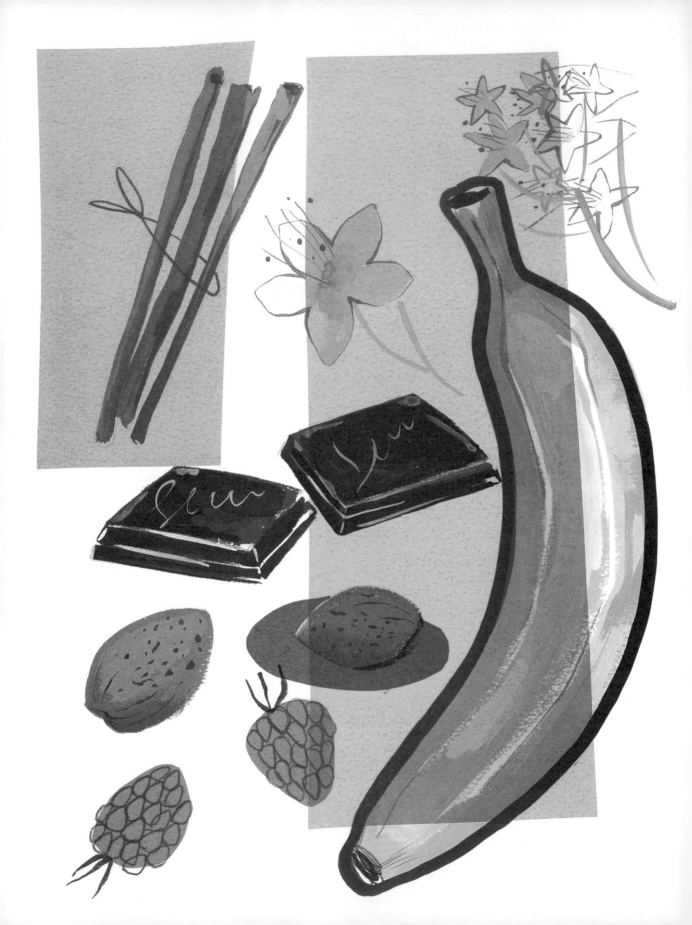

love eating out, but invariably the pudding course doesn't quite hold up to the rest of the menu. There is a sameness about what's on offer – for instance, you'll always find crème brûlée. It's one of my favourites, but I still see it too often! I love puds so much that when I plan the menus at Kinloch I start with the puddings and work back – and the recipes in this chapter reflect this. There are simple, seasonal ones, such as Damsons with Yogurt Cream (page 207), and rich, lavish ones, such as the Bûche de Noël on page 234. There are spoon-and-fork substitutes, like Dark Chocolate Ginger Biscuits (page 238) – lovely with a cup of coffee at the end of lunch or supper – and ices, of course: the rich, indulgent Pecan Caramel Vanilla Ice Cream (page 241), the sophisticated Marrons Glacés and Maple Syrup Semi-freddo (page 240), and the lighter, fragrant Redcurrant and Lemon Water Ice (page 245). The elaborate choco-laty cake-based puddings, like Rich Dark Chocolate and Almond Cake with Chocolate Cream (page 232) and Dark Chocolate Cappuccino Mousse Cake (page 230), are showstoppers at dinner parties. There are fruity puds, too: Strawberries with Amaretto, with Amaretto Syllabub (page 201), wonderful in June, and in the autumn, Pumpkin Pie with Orange Pastry and Caramelized Pecans (page 218).

The one thing that all these puds have in common is that they can be made entirely, or mostly, well in advance, sometimes by weeks, if they're frozen, but at least a day or several hours ahead. I hope you enjoy them.

Praline and vanilla crêpes

with butterscotch sauce

There is a wonderful hotel in Salzburg that feels like a home – albeit with a superb chef in the kitchen! That was where I first sampled this sublime combination of flavours and textures. It's one of their best-known puddings and I have tried here to reconstruct it. The batter for crêpes of all types can be made a couple of days in advance, providing that you stir it up well before you cook the crêpes on the day you plan to eat them. You can whip the cream hours in advance – it must be double cream, not whipping, which, with its reduced fat content, tends to 'fall' if whipped too soon. The praline and the sauce can both be made 2–3 days ahead. Don't be put off by the length of the recipe – the various elements are all quick, easy and fun to make. All that remains is to assemble the crêpes and warm up the sauce before your guests arrive.

Serves 6

for the crêpes
4 oz/110 g plain flour
2 large eggs
½ pint/300 ml *full-fat* milk
½ tsp liquid vanilla extract *or* 1 level tsp powdered vanilla extract
1 tbsp caster sugar
butter

for the filling
1 pint/600 ml double cream
½ tsp liquid vanilla extract *or* ½ tsp powdered vanilla extract

for the praline
butter to grease a baking tray
3 oz/75 g flaked *or* nibbed almonds
8 oz/225 g granulated sugar

for the butterscotch sauce
6 oz/175 g granulated sugar
2 oz/50 g soft dark brown sugar
1 pint/600 ml water
4 oz/110 g butter, cut into bits
½ pint/300 ml double cream
½ tsp liquid vanilla extract *or* ½ tsp powdered vanilla extract

To make the crêpes, put all the ingredients, except the butter, into a food-processor and whiz to a smooth batter. Leave it to stand for at least 30 minutes and up to 2 days. Stir it well before you make the crêpes. To cook the crêpes, put a piece of butter, about the size of a thumbnail, into a small non-stick frying pan over a moderate heat. When the butter has melted and the pan is hot, pour in a small amount of batter, tipping and tilting the pan as you do so. The heat of the pan will seal the batter into a thin, even film over the base. Cook for a few seconds then slip your thumbs under the crêpe, flip it over, and cook it for a few seconds on the other side. Tip the cooked crêpe on to a large plastic or cloth-covered wooden tray to cool. This amount of batter should produce 12 crêpes. When the cooked crêpes have cooled (2–3 minutes), stack them. When all the batter has been used, cover the stack with a cloth to prevent the air making them stale.

For the filling, whip the cream with the vanilla. Keep the bowl, covered, in the fridge.

To make the praline, butter a baking tray thoroughly. Put the almonds into a heavy-based saucepan or sauté pan over a moderate heat. Shake the pan until the almonds are lightly toasted and biscuit-coloured. Add the sugar to the pan, and continue to shake – never stir – until the sugar begins to dissolve. Don't try to hurry this along by raising the heat: burnt caramel tastes so bitter and acrid that you will have to start again. Whe you have a molten rich brown caramel pour it on to the buttered baking tray and leave it to set. When it is cold lay a sheet of baking parchment over the nutty caramel – this helps prevent bits flying all over your kitchen – and gently bash it with the end of a rolling-pin to crumbs, as coarse or as fine as you choose. I like mine medium-fine so that the nutty texture, one of the – many! – attractions of this pudding, remains intact. Spoon the praline into an airtight container to store for 2 to 3 days until you assemble the crêpes.

To make the sauce, put all of the sugar into a saucepan with the water. Over a moderate heat, let it dissolve in the water, shaking the pan gently from time to time. When it has completely dissolved, let the liquid come to the boil, then simmer for 10 minutes. Take the pan off the heat and whisk in the butter, a little at a time. Lastly, stir in the cream and the vanilla. Store it in a screw-topped jar. It will separate, with the sugar syrup at the bottom, until you reheat it. To reheat, boil the sauce for 2 minutes, then keep it warm for serving.

. . . .

To assemble the crêpes, put a spoonful of praline on a crêpe, then a spoonful of vanilla cream. Roll it up in a cigar shape, or fold it in half to form a half-moon. Continue until all of the crêpes are used up. Put a small amount of warm butterscotch sauce on each plate, with 2 crêpes – or, if you prefer, hand the warm sauce separately in a jug.

Strawberries with Amaretto

with Amaretto syllabub

I loathe sticky drinks – except Amaretto, which I find utterly delicious. In this simple recipe the sliced strawberries are steeped in Amaretto, and served with an Amaretto syllabub spooned over them. It benefits from being made a day in advance, to give the Amaretto flavour time to intensify. I like to serve it with the delicious bitter-almond Amaretti biscuits, which are available from most supermarkets and delicatessens.

Serves 6

**1½ lb/675 g strawberries, sliced *or* chopped
8 tbsp Amaretto
1 pint/600 ml double cream
2 large egg whites**

Put the strawberries into a fairly wide dish, and spoon over them 6 tablespoons of the Amaretto. Mix thoroughly, and leave in a cool place, but not the fridge, for 3–4 hours, or longer. Put the cream and the egg whites together into a bowl and whisk them until they are fairly thick. Strain the juice from the strawberries, and whip it with the remaining Amaretto into the cream.

. . . .

Just before serving, divide the strawberries between 6 large glasses or goblets, then spoon the syllabub over the top. If you are not ready to serve them at once, leave in a cool place – not the fridge, though – until you are ready.

Lemon crêpes

with crushed raspberry cream

This is an elegant and convenient way to eat raspberries in the middle of their season – when I want to do more with them than heap them on a serving plate, dust them with sugar and serve them with cream. After a few days, I find myself looking for recipes to use them up, and there are many because raspberries are so versatile. But lemon really brings out their flavour. Make the crêpe batter a couple of days in advance, and keep it in a covered jug in the fridge. Cook the crêpes, whip the cream and crush the raspberries in the morning of the day you plan to eat them, and fill the crêpes several hours before serving.

Serves 6

for the crêpes
4 oz/110 g plain flour
2 large eggs
½ pint/300 ml *full-fat* milk
1 tbsp caster sugar
finely grated zest of 1½ lemons
a few drops of liquid vanilla extract *or* ½ tsp powdered vanilla extract
butter

for the filling
¾ pint/450 ml double cream, whipped
1 lb/450 g raspberries, crushed
2 oz/50 g caster sugar
finely grated zest of 1 lemon

First make the crêpe batter: put all the ingredients, except the butter, into a food-processor or blender and whiz until smooth. Leave the batter in a jug, covered in the fridge, for at least 30 minutes and up to 2 days. Give it a good stir before you use it. To cook the crêpes, put a piece of butter, about the size of a thumbnail, into a small non-stick frying pan over a moderate heat. When it has melted and the pan is hot, pour in a small amount of batter, tipping and tilting the pan to get an even film of across the base. Cook for a few seconds, then slip your thumbs under the crêpe, flip it over, and cook for a few seconds on the other side. Put it on to a large plastic tray, or a wooden tray or board covered it with a cloth, to cool. Repeat until all the batter is used up – you should end up with 12 crêpes. When the crêpes are cold, stack them and cover them with a cloth.

· ·

To assemble the crêpes, stir together the whipped cream, crushed raspberries, sugar and lemon zest and spread some over a crêpe. Roll it up into a cigar shape, and put it on a serving plate. Repeat with the rest. You can roll them up several hours before serving, but cover the dish and its contents with a cloth to prevent the air making the filled crêpes stale and leathery. Dust the crêpes with a spoonful of sieved icing sugar immediately before serving.

Old-fashioned baked caramel vanilla creams

One of my favourites of all the puddings we make at Kinloch. It's soft in texture, with a richness that is pure luxury – rather like eating cashmere! The crisp caramel chips scattered over the whipped cream make a lovely contrast. You can make the caramel 2–3 days ahead, and the creams 1 day in advance.

Serves 6

butter to grease the ramekins
8 egg yolks
6 tbsp caster sugar
½ tsp liquid vanilla extract *or* ½ tsp powdered vanilla extract, *or* scrape the insides of 2 vanilla pods
1 pint/600 ml double cream, plus ½ pint/300 ml double cream, whipped, to garnish

for the
caramel chips

8 oz/225 g granulated sugar
butter

Preheat the oven to 200°F/100°C/Gas Mark ¼.

Butter thoroughly 6 large ramekins and put them into a roasting tin. In a bowl, beat the egg yolks with the caster sugar and vanilla powder (use liquid extract if you would rather, but these tend to taste of the alcohol in which the vanilla is preserved rather than the vanilla) and stir in the 1 pint/600 ml cream. Pour the mixture into a jug, and then into the ramekins. Then pour near-boiling water around the ramekins in the roasting tin to come half-way up their sides, and bake in the cool oven (top left oven in a 4-door Aga) for 1 hour. Gently press the centre of one of the ramekins: it should not feel wobbly. If it does, continue to cook the creams for a further 20–30 minutes. Take them out and keep them, covered, in a cool place until you need them.

To make the caramel, butter a baking tray thoroughly. Put the sugar into a heavy-bottomed saucepan over moderate heat. Gently shake the pan until the sugar has dissolved. Do not stir the melting caramel, and don't try to hurry it. When you have a molten dark brown caramel, pour it on to the baking tray and leave it to cool completely. Then cover the caramel with a sheet of baking parchment – which helps prevent the chips of caramel from flying all over your kitchen – and bash it with the end of a rolling-pin into chips as small or as large as you choose. Store them in an airtight container, away from any moisture.

. . . .

To serve, put a dollop of whipped cream on top of each vanilla cream, and scatter over a generous amount of caramel chips. Serve the ramekins on small plates, with a teaspoon on each.

Lemon cream rice

with griottes

Every storecupboard should contain a couple of jars of griottes, or griottines: cherries preserved in Kirsch. A sniff of the jar positively lifts the spirits, but they are useful, delicious and easily dressed up with vanilla ice cream and a warm dark chocolate sauce, or put into a chocolate meringue with whipped cream. But they are a most uplifting accompaniment to this lemon- and vanilla-flavoured creamy rice. You can't eat many – you'd end up on the floor! The rice cream can be made a day in advance.

Serves 6

2 oz/50 g round-grain pudding rice
1½ pints/900 ml full-fat milk
3 oz/75 g caster sugar
½ tsp liquid vanilla extract *or* **½ tsp powdered vanilla extract**
finely grated zest of 2 lemons
½ pint/300 ml double cream, whipped to soft peaks
1 pint/600 ml griottes *or* **griottines**

Put the rice, milk and sugar into a saucepan over a moderate heat and cook gently, stirring occasionally, for 30 minutes, or until each grain is soft. Add the vanilla and the lemon zest, then take the pan off the heat, and leave it to cool.

When the lemon rice is cold, fold in the whipped cream, and pour it into a pretty serving dish or bowl. Put the cherries into another bowl, and serve.

Damsons with yogurt cream

A pudding for early autumn! Damsons are one of my favourite fruits. This is an old recipe from the seventies, but then we made this with grapes. However, you can use any fruit under the simple cream and yogurt top, although I think damsons are by far the most interesting. It must be made a day in advance.

Serves 6

2 lb/900 g damsons
¼ pint/150 ml water
about 6 oz/175 g sugar, *or* to taste
½ pint/300 ml double cream, whipped to soft peaks
½ pint/300 ml best Greek yogurt
6 tbsp golden granulated sugar

Take a saucepan that isn't made of aluminium and put in the damsons with the water. Cover the pan and cook them over a gentle heat until some of the skins burst. Take them off and stir in the sugar until it has dissolved. Let the damsons cool. Then – and this is worth the small amount of time it takes – with a slotted spoon, lift out a spoonful of damsons and fork out the stones. Put the stoned damsons into a serving bowl. Repeat until all the damsons are stone-free. Fold together the whipped cream and yoghurt and cover the damsons with it. Cover the cream with the golden granulated sugar, and leave it overnight.

Toasted almond mousse

An unusual mousse, because it has to be put into a wide, shallow dish, not a bowl, so that you can brûlé *the top with a blowtorch, caramelizing the sugar and toasting the nuts. The crunchy surface provides a good contrast of texture with the silky mousse. Delicious! You can make the mousse a day in advance, and it takes only 2–3 minutes to scatter over the nuts and sugar and finish off with the blowtorch. Hold the blowtorch well away – too close and the sugar burns. About 12 in/30 cm is fine.*

Serves 6

¼ pint/150 ml cold water

½ tsp almond extract

3 leaves Costa gelatine, soaked in cold water for 10 minutes, *or*

   2 tsp powdered gelatine, soaked in 3 tbsp cold water

4 large eggs, separated

4 oz/110 g caster sugar, plus a pinch

½ pint/300 ml double cream, whipped and chilled

4 oz/110 g flaked almonds

4 tbsp granulated sugar

Put the water into a saucepan with the almond extract over a moderate heat. When it is hot, but not boiling, drop in the gelatine and gently shake the pan until it has dissolved. Let it cool. Whisk the egg yolks with the caster sugar until very pale and thick, then whisk in the cooled gelatine liquid. Fold in the cold whipped cream. With a scrupulously clean whisk, beat the egg whites with a pinch of salt until they are stiff. With a large metal spoon fold these quickly and thoroughly through the creamy mixture. Pour and scrape into a wide shallow dish. Cover it, and leave it in a cool place, or the fridge, overnight.

. . . .

To finish the mousse – you can do this several hours in advance – scatter the flaked almonds as evenly as possible over the surface, then the granulated sugar. With a blowtorch – from Lakeland or an Aga shop – *brûlé* the surface until the nuts are toasted and the sugar melted into a light caramel.

Cardamom and cinnamon cream

with crushed strawberries or raspberries

These spices are so good with either strawberries or raspberries – we tend to overlook spices as a flavour enhancer for soft fruits. This pudding has to be made a day in advance and kept, covered, in the fridge until 30 minutes before serving. You can caramelize the surface several hours before eating. **Serves 6**

1 pint/600 ml double cream
1 cinnamon stick
3 cardamom seeds, bashed, husks removed
6 large egg yolks
2 oz/50 g caster sugar
1½ lb/675 g strawberries *or* raspberries, crushed
3 tbsp granulated sugar, golden if you like – you may need more

Put the cream, with the cinnamon and cardamom, into a saucepan and heat it until it is scalded. Take the pan off the heat, and leave it for several hours to infuse. In a bowl beat together the egg yolks and caster sugar until they are pale and thick. Reheat the cream, and pour it through a sieve into the yolks and sugar, stirring well. Now put the bowl into a microwave oven on high for 1 minute, take it out and stir it well with a balloon whisk. Put it back into the microwave and cook for 1 minute on medium. Take it out, stir well, and put it back for 30 seconds on medium. Continue until the creamy custard has thickened. Exactly how long it takes depends on the bowl you are using – Pyrex takes about 4 minutes; other materials might take as long as 8. (Or put the bowl over a saucepan of boiling water and stir it until it thickens. This is a fine method, but it takes 40–45 minutes.)

Put the crushed berries into a bowl. Cover with the thickened cream, and leave to cool.

. . . .

When cold, and a skin has formed, cover the surface with the sugar then, with a blowtorch held 12 in/30 cm away, caramelize the surface. In the absence of a blowtorch, heat the grill to red-hot, and put the bowl or dish under it until the sugar has melted to a pale caramel – first make sure that the bowl or dish will withstand heat.

Warm fudge apple slices

with spiced iced cream

I love cold and warm dishes together. And this rich, sticky combination is easy and convenient to make. The Spiced Iced Cream will freeze well for up to 6 weeks, the fudge sauce can be made 3 days in advance, and the finished apple slices will keep warm without spoiling for ages – a couple of hours, covered, in a low oven.

Serves 6

for the spiced iced cream

2 large egg whites
3 oz/75 g icing sugar, sieved
½ pint/300 ml double cream
1 rounded tsp powdered cinnamon
1 tsp finely ground black pepper
a grating of nutmeg
½ tsp powdered vanilla extract

for the fudge apple slices

4 oz/110 g butter
4 oz/110 g soft brown sugar, light or dark
½ pint/300 ml double cream
½ tsp powdered vanilla extract, *or* a few drops of vanilla extract
8 best eating apples, peeled, cored and sliced – British-grown for their character, please

Make the iced cream: whisk the egg whites until they are stiff, then whisk in the icing sugar, a little at a time. When it is all incorporated and you have a stiff meringue, whip the cream, adding the cinnamon, black pepper, nutmeg and vanilla, until it is in soft peaks. With a large metal spoon fold together the mixtures and freeze in a solid polythene container – there is no need to beat this iced cream as it freezes. Take the container from the freezer and put it into the fridge when you start the meal.

Make the fudge sauce: put the butter, sugar, cream and vanilla into a saucepan over a moderate heat. Stir until the butter has melted and the sugar dissolved, then let the sauce boil for 3–5 minutes – the longer you boil the sauce, the thicker it becomes. Cool and keep in the fridge to reheat later. It keeps for up to 3 days.

puddings

Reheat the sauce, and add the sliced apples. Cook them gently for 4–5 minutes then pour everything into a serving dish. Keep it warm in a low oven until you need it.

Serve a spoonful or two of the apples in their sauce with a spoonful of the iced cream either beside the fudge-sauced apples or on top. Dip a large spoon in hot water for a few seconds to make serving the iced cream easier.

Aromatic baked raisin and ginger cream

An aromatic, rich, velvety-smooth cream. The better the raisins you use, the more sumptuous will be the result. Lexia are nearly the best, but semi-dried grapes are the last word in raisins. If it is easier for you, make the creams a day in advance, but don't serve them straight from the fridge: leave them at room temperature for at least an hour, when the fragrant cardamom will be at its most intense. Remember before you start that the raisins have to be soaked overnight before you use them.

Serves 6

6 oz/175 g best-quality raisins
3 tbsp Crabbie's Green Ginger Wine
1 pint/600 ml double cream
3 cardamom seeds, bashed, husks removed
6 large egg yolks
1 tbsp caster sugar

Soak the raisins in the ginger wine overnight.

Preheat the oven to 250°F/125°C/Gas Mark ½.

Put 6 ramekins into a roasting tin. Put the cream and the cardamom seeds into a saucepan over a moderate heat. Cook until tiny bubbles form around the edge of the pan then take it off. In a bowl, beat the yolks with the caster sugar. Strain the heated cream into the egg mixture, and stir together thoroughly. Divide the raisins between the ramekins and pour over the cream mixture. Fill a roasting tin to a depth of about 1 in/2.5 cm with nearly-boiling water. Bake in the slow oven (top left oven in a 4-door Aga), for 1 hour, or until the custards no longer wobble in the centres – the last part to set. If after 1 hour they are a bit wobbly, continue cooking for a further 10 minutes, or until they feel gently firm. Take the tin out of the oven.

. . . .

You can serve these creams just warm, but I prefer them cooled.

Baked ginger pears

with oatmeal fudge crumble

A warm pudding is deeply comforting, especially when accompanied by vanilla ice cream. You can substitute apples for the pears, but I think ginger is especially good with the latter.

Serves 6

10 ripe Conference pears, or more, if they are small
6 pieces stem ginger, drained of syrup and chopped
finely grated zest of 1 lemon

4 oz/110 g butter   *for the crumble*
4 oz/110 g Demerara sugar
2 oz/50 g porridge oats
6 oz/175 g pinhead oatmeal
½ tsp powdered vanilla extract, *or* liquid extract

First, make the crumble mixture. Melt the butter in a sauté pan and stir in the sugar, porridge oats and pinhead oatmeal. Add the vanilla, and cook over a moderate heat, stirring lazily, for several minutes.

Peel, core and slice the pears into an ovenproof dish. Scatter over the chopped ginger and the lemon zest. Spoon over the crumble mixture. Set aside until you are ready to bake it.

. . . .

Bake the crumble in a preheated moderate oven, 350°F/180°C/Gas Mark 4 (bottom right oven in a 4-door Aga), for 25–30 minutes, or until the top is golden brown and crisp. You can keep this warm for an hour or longer in a low oven.

Coffee cream pie

with rich chocolate biscuit pastry

The combined flavours of coffee and chocolate are so good – and heavenly in this torte. You can make the chocolate pie crust up to a week ahead, keep it in a thick polythene bag and make the filling a day in advance. Put it into the crust several hours before you plan to eat it. When grating chocolate, hold it wrapped in a double thickness of foil to stop it melting in your hand. Use a potato peeler for larger curls.

Serves 6

for the rich biscuit pastry case
- **4 oz/110 g butter, hard from the fridge, diced**
- **5 oz/150 g plain flour**
- **1 oz/25 g cocoa powder**
- **1 oz/25 g icing sugar**
- **½ tsp liquid vanilla extract, *or* ½ tsp powdered vanilla extract**

for the filling
- **1 pint/600 ml single cream**
- **2 tsp coffee essence**
- **6 large egg yolks**
- **4 oz/110 g caster sugar**
- **2 leaves Costa gelatine, soaked in cold water, *or* 2 tsp powdered gelatine, soaked in 3 tbsp cold water**
- **½ pint/300 ml double cream, whipped**
- **3 tbsp best-quality – minimum 70% cocoa solids – dark chocolate, coarsely grated**

To make the base, put the ingredients into a food-processor and whiz until the mixture resembles fine crumbs. Press them firmly around the sides and base of a 9-in/22-cm flan dish or tin. Put it into the fridge for at least 1 hour. Bake in a preheated moderate oven, 350°F/180°C/Gas Mark (bottom right oven in a 4-door Aga), for 20–25 minutes, or until the pastry is just beginning to shrink away from the sides of the dish. If it slips down during cooking, press it back with a metal spoon.

For the filling, heat the single cream in a saucepan with the coffee essence until it is scalding. Meanwhile, in a bowl beat the egg yolks with the caster sugar. Pour the scalding coffee cream into the egg yolks and mix thoroughly. Now put the bowl into a microwave oven for 1 minute on high, take it out and stir hard with a balloon whisk; put it back and cook for 30 seconds on medium, take it out again and stir well. Repeat, cooking for 30 seconds on medium and stirring, until the custard is the consistency of thick cream. Otherwise put the bowl over a saucepan of simmering water, and stir the custard until it thickens, 40–45 minutes. (You need to be patient.) Then stir in the gelatine until it has dissolved. Leave the custard to cool and begin to set. Fold together the setting custard and the whipped cream, with the grated chocolate.

Several hours before serving, pile the filling into the baked chocolate pastry case.

Orange tart with ginger pastry

and ginger vanilla crème pâtissière

This is particularly good in the winter when blood oranges are available. They look so striking, streaked with red, and they taste superb. But, of course, you can make it at any time of the year, with any type of sweet orange. You can make the pastry base several days in advance and keep it in a thick polythene bag, and the ginger vanilla crème pâtissière a day ahead. Then all you need to do, several hours before serving, is slice the oranges, melt the jelly and assemble the tart. Easy!

Serves 6

for the pastry
- **4 oz/110 g butter, hard from the fridge, diced**
- **6 oz/175 g plain flour**
- **1 tsp powdered ginger**
- **1 tbsp icing sugar**

for the crème pâtissière
- **1 pint/600 ml single cream**
- **5 large egg yolks (keep the whites for making meringues)**
- **4 oz/110 g caster sugar**
- **1 tsp liquid vanilla extract *or* 1 tsp vanilla powder**
- **6 pieces stem ginger, drained and finely chopped**
- **2 leaves Costa gelatine, soaked in cold water, *or* 2 tsp powdered gelatine, soaked in 1 tbsp cold water**

to finish the tart
- **1 x 15-oz/400-g pot shredless orange jellied marmalade**
- **4–6 oranges, peeled and sliced – flick out any pips**

First, make the pastry. Put the ingredients into a food-processor and whiz to fine crumbs. Firmly press them around the sides and over the base of a 9-in/22-cm flan tin or dish and put it into the fridge for 1 hour. Bake in a preheated moderate oven, 350°F/180°C/ Gas Mark 4 (bottom right oven in a 4-door Aga), for 20–25 minutes, or until the pastry is just beginning to shrink away from the sides of the dish. Should it slip down during cooking, take a metal spoon, push it back up and bake for another couple of minutes. Take it out and let it cool.

For the ginger crème pâtissière, put the cream into a saucepan and heat it gently. Meanwhile beat together the egg yolks, sugar, vanilla and ginger. Pour on the hot cream, and mix thoroughly. The quickest way to cook the custard is in a microwave oven. Put the bowl into the oven on high for 1 minute, take it out and stir it vigorously with a balloon whisk. Put it back and cook for 1 minute on medium, stir and cook again for 30 seconds on medium. It will thicken, but how long this takes depends on the microwave oven – they vary – and whether you cook in Pyrex, ceramic or rigid plastic bowls. Pyrex is the quickest. So, continue to cook for 30 seconds at a time, on medium, until it is as thick as you like it. (In the absence of a microwave oven, put the bowl over a saucepan of boiling water and stir it until it thickens. This is a fine method, but it takes 40–45 minutes.) When it is ready take the bowl out of the oven, drop in the gelatine, and stir until it has dissolved. Cool the crème pâtissière until it starts to set, then spoon it evenly over the baked pastry.

To finish the tart, melt the marmalade in a saucepan over moderate heat. Arrange the sliced oranges over the crème pâtissière. Spoon the melted jellied marmalade over the entire surface of the tart, pastry edges, the lot, and leave it to set.

Pumpkin pie with spiced orange pastry

and caramelized pecans

Many, many Hallowe'ens ago, an Australian friend taught me an invaluable lesson. In vain had I steamed pumpkin flesh or simmered it in water, but no matter how I flavoured it it tasted vile. She told me always to cook it in milk, and my pumpkin pies were transformed. This pie is convenient because the pastry base can be made up to a week ahead, but it must be kept in a thick polythene bag. The pumpkin can be cooked 2 days in advance and the filling mixture a day ahead, but the pie must be baked on the same day it is to be eaten – in the morning for the evening is fine.

Serves 6

for the pastry
4 oz/110 g butter, hard from the fridge, diced
5 oz/150 g plain flour
1 oz/25 g icing sugar
finely grated zest of 2 oranges
1 rounded tsp powdered cinnamon
a grating of nutmeg

for the pecans
8 oz/225 g granulated sugar
4 oz/110 g pecans

for the filling
about 1 lb/450 g pumpkin flesh
about 2 pints/1.2 litres milk to cover the pumpkin
1 cinnamon stick
2 large eggs
2 large egg yolks
4 oz/110 g soft brown sugar, light or dark
½ pint/300 ml double cream
½ tsp liquid vanilla extract, *or* ½ tsp powdered vanilla extract

Put the pastry ingredients into a food-processor and whiz to the texture of fine crumbs. Press them firmly around the sides and base of a 9-in/22-cn flan dish or tin. Put it into the fridge for at least 1 hour. Bake in a preheated moderate oven, 350°F/180°C/Gas Mark 4 (bottom right oven in a 4-door Aga), for 20–25 minutes, or until the pastry just begins to shrink away from the sides of the dish. If it slips down the sides during cooking, press it back with a metal spoon.

To make the caramelized pecans, line a baking tray with baking parchment. Put the sugar into a heavy-bottomed saucepan over a moderate heat and shake the pan as the sugar dissolves, and becomes a dark rich caramel. *Do not try to hurry this process or stir the sugar.* Add the pecans, stir over the heat, and shake them into the caramel. Pour it on to the lined baking tray, then leave it to cool and harden. Then cover it with a sheet of baking parchment (to help prevent the caramelized nuts from flying over your kitchen) and bash it with the end of a rolling-pin to break it up a bit.

To make the pie filling, preheat the oven to 350°F/180°C/Gas Mark 4. Put the pumpkin in a saucepan with the milk and cinnamon and cook it until it is soft. Strain off the milk, put the pumpkin into a food-processor and whiz. Beat together the eggs and yolks, then whiz them with the sugar, cream and vanilla into the pumpkin. Pour the mixture into the baked pastry shell, and bake in the moderate oven (bottom right oven in a 4-door Aga) for 15–20 minutes, or until the centre feels just firm and not wobbly. Take the pie out of the oven, and cover the surface with the caramelized pecans.

. . . .

Serve with whipped cream or thick crème fraiche.

Walnut and orange roulade

Walnuts benefit hugely from being chopped then dry-fried. (All nuts stale, but none more so than walnuts, which tend to become bitter. The best way to store nuts is in the freezer.) This soft-textured roulade, with toasted walnuts and vanilla, is delicious with its orange-cream filling. It can be made, filled and rolled up in the morning for eating that evening. The oranges can be cooked a couple of days ahead of making the roulade.

Serves 6

4 large eggs, separated
6 oz/175 g caster sugar
½ tsp liquid vanilla extract *or* vanilla powder
3 oz/75 g walnuts, chopped, dry-fried and cooled
pinch of salt
icing sugar, sieved

for the filling **2 sweet oranges, sliced *or* very finely chopped**
1 tbsp caster sugar
½ tsp liquid vanilla extract *or* vanilla powder
½ pint/300 ml double cream, whipped fairly stiffly

Preheat the oven to 350°F/180°C/Gas Mark 4.

Line a 9 x 12 in/22 x 30 cm baking tray or Swiss roll tin with baking parchment. Put a dab of butter in each corner to anchor it. Whisk the egg yolks with the caster sugar and vanilla until they are pale and very thick. Then add the chopped walnuts, mixing them in well. In another bowl, using a clean whisk, beat the egg whites with the salt (which gives increased volume) until they are stiff, then fold them thoroughly with a large metal spoon through the walnut mixture. Pour it into the lined tin, smooth it even, and bake in the moderate oven (bottom right oven in a 4-door Aga) for 20 minutes, or until the cooked roulade is just shrinking away from the sides and feels springy when you press it gently in the centre. Take the tin out of the oven and cover it with a cloth. Leave it to cool.

Meanwhile, make the filling. Put the oranges into a saucepan, and cover with cold water. Bring it to a simmer over a moderate heat, and cook the oranges gently for 15 minutes. Stick a fork into a piece, and if it feels tender, take the oranges off and strain them. If the peel feels stiff, continue to simmer for a further 5 minutes, then strain them. Stir the sugar and vanilla into the whipped cream. Set aside.

To assemble the roulade, lay a sheet of baking parchment on a work surface, and dust it liberally with sieved icing sugar. Tip the cooked roulade face down on the icing sugar, and carefully peel the paper off the back of the roulade, tearing it in strips parallel to the roulade – this avoids tearing the roulade up with the paper. Spread the vanilla whipped cream over the surface. Strew the cooked sliced oranges over the cream. Roll up the roulade, lengthways, and slip it off the paper on to a serving plate.

. . . .

To serve, slice the roulade thickly, and this is easiest done with a serrated knife. Dust with icing sugar again before serving if you like.

Apple, almond and soured cream tart

This is an excellent apple tart. I like to serve it warm, but it is just as good cold. The pastry can be made several days in advance, providing that you keep it airtight in a thick polythene bag. The filling can be made and baked several hours in advance, in the morning, for eating that evening.

Serves 6

for the pastry base
4 oz/110 g butter, hard from the fridge, diced
1 oz/25 g icing sugar
4 oz/110 g ground almonds
2 oz/50 g flour
½ tsp almond extract

for the filling
6 eating apples, e.g. Cox's in season, peeled, cored, sliced and brushed with lemon juice
juice of 1 lemon
½ tsp liquid vanilla extract or powdered vanilla
½ pint/300 ml single cream
1 large egg
2 egg yolks
3 oz/75 g caster sugar

Put all the pastry ingredients into a food-processor and whiz to the texture of fairly fine crumbs. Press them firmly around the sides and base of a 9in/22-cm flan dish or tin. Put it into the fridge for at least 1 hour, then bake in a preheated moderate oven, 350°F/180°C/Gas Mark 4 (bottom right oven in a 4-door Aga), for 20 minutes, or until the pastry is light golden. If it should slip down the sides during cooking, press it back with a metal spoon.

Arrange the apple slices over the baked pastry base. In a bowl stir the lemon juice and vanilla into the cream. Beat the egg with the yolks, and then beat in the sugar. Stir in the cream mixture, and pour it all into the pastry case, over the apples. Bake for 15–20 minutes, or until the cream is no longer wobbling in the centre when you gently shake the dish – the centre is the last to set.

. . . .

Serve at room temperature, or keep it warm in a low oven.

Muscat-jellied fruit terrine

The base for this terrine is a syrup flavoured with blackcurrant leaves, which must sound strange to those not familiar with old-fashioned water-ices. The leaves taste of muscat grapes – a truly exquisite flavour that goes well with all summer fruits. If you like, you could serve it with a puréed-fruit sauce, sieved to achieve a velvety, seed-free texture.

Serves 6

8 oz/225 g granulated sugar *for the*
1 pint/600 ml cold water *blackcurrant-leaf*
pared zest and juice of 1 lemon *syrup*
2 large handfuls blackcurrant leaves, stripped from the stalks

6 leaves Costa gelatine, *or* 1½ sachets powdered gelatine *for the terrine*
1¾ pints/750 ml blackcurrant-leaf syrup (see above), the amount made up with cold water
1½ lb/675 g any soft fruit, mixed *or* 1 variety

To make the syrup, put the sugar, water and lemon rind into a saucepan over a moderate heat and let the sugar dissolve. Then bring it to the boil, and continue to boil, not too furiously, for 4–5 minutes. Take the pan off the heat, plunge in the blackcurrant leaves and add the lemon juice – in that order. Leave the syrup for several hours to cool and infuse with the taste of the leaves. Then strain it, pressing down on the leaves to extract as much syrup as you can.

To make the terrine, line a terrine or loaf tin with clingfilm. Soak the leaf gelatine for at least 10 minutes in cold water, or powdered gelatine in 3 tablespoons cold water until it is spongy. Warm a small amount of the blackcurrant-leaf syrup and water, and drop in the soaked gelatine leaves – they will dissolve almost immediately. Otherwise put the spongy gelatine into the warm liquid and shake the pan gently until the granules have dissolved completely. Stir the gelatine liquid in to the rest of the syrup and water.

Put the fruit into the lined terrine, and carefully pour the liquid over it. Leave it to set overnight in the fridge, covered with clingfilm.

. . . .

Turn the terrine out on to a serving plate, and slice thickly to serve.

Lemon and elderflower syllabub

with marinated blueberries

The syllabub has a lovely haunting flavour, and is quick to prepare. Both parts have to be made several hours in advance, if not the previous day. It is simplicity itself.

Serves 6

for the blueberries
1½ lb/675 g blueberries
finely grated zest and juice of 2 lemons (well washed first)
½ pint/300 ml elderflower cordial

for the syllabub
1 pint/600 ml double cream
3 tbsp elderflower cordial
finely grated zest of 2 lemons, juice of 1
2 large egg whites
2 oz/50 g icing sugar, sieved

Put the blueberries into a bowl with the lemon zest and juice and the elderflower cordial. Mix together thoroughly, cover the bowl, and leave for several hours or overnight.

For the syllabub, whip the cream with the elderflower cordial and lemon juice, then stir in the zest. Take a clean whisk, and beat the egg whites. When they are fairly stiff, whisk in the icing sugar a small amount at a time. Fold together the cream mixture and the whisked whites and set aside.

. . . .

To serve, divide the marinated blueberries between 6 large glasses, then heap some syllabub on top. Alternatively, serve them separately, with the syllabub piled in one bowl and the marinated blueberries in another.

Lemon and elderflower syllabub with marinated blueberries

Raspberry tart

with brown sugar and toasted pecan pastry

Although I use raspberries here, you can substitute any other berry or currant you choose. The rich and crunchy pastry base can be made 5 days in advance. Store, when cold, in a thick polythene bag.

Serves 6

4 oz/110 g butter, hard from the fridge, diced   *for the pastry*
5oz/155 g plain flour
2 oz/50 g Demerara *or* golden granulated sugar
3 oz/75 g pecan nuts, broken up and dry-fried

1½ lb/675 g raspberries   *for the filling*
finely grated zest and juice of 1 lemon
about 4 oz/110 g sugar, to taste
2 rounded tsp arrowroot, mixed with 1 tbsp cold water

Preheat the oven to 350°F/180°C/Gas Mark 4.

To make the pastry, put the butter, flour and sugar into a food-processor and whiz until you have fine crumbs. Then add the toasted pecan nuts, and whiz very briefly to incorporate them and break them down a little. Press the mixture firmly around the sides and base of a 9-in/22-cm flan dish, put it into the fridge for at least 1 hour, then bake in the moderate oven (bottom right oven in a 4-door Aga) for 15–20 minutes.

For the filling, put the raspberries into a saucepan with the lemon juice and zest. Cover with a lid, and cook gently over a low heat until the juices run from the raspberries. Then stir in the sugar carefully, so that you don't break up the berries more than you can help. Mix some of the hot juice into the arrowroot mixture, then stir this carefully into the contents of the pan until it bubbles. Take the pan off the heat, let it cool, then pour the raspberry mixture into the baked pastry case.

. . . .

Serve with vanilla whipped cream or crème fraiche.

Raspberry tart with brown sugar and toasted pecan pastry

Pistachio meringue cake

with orange and vanilla cream

I love all types of nutty meringue, almond, hazelnut, and walnut, but pistachios are more unusual and just as good. The meringue rounds can be made up to a week in advance, and kept in an airtight container. The orange and vanilla-flavoured cream will sit happily in a covered bowl in the fridge for several hours. The cake is best assembled a few hours ahead, too – in fact, it will be easier to cut if you do.

Serves 6

for the meringue
4 large egg whites
8 oz/225 g caster sugar
3 oz/75 g pistachios, weighed when shelled, dry-fried for 5 minutes and chopped

for the filling
¾ pint/450 ml double cream
finely grated zest of 2 oranges and juice of 1
1 tbsp icing sugar, sieved, plus 2 tsp for dusting, sieved
½ tsp powdered vanilla extract *or* liquid extract

First make the meringues. Preheat the oven to 225°F/110°C/ Gas Mark ¼. Line two 9-in/22-cm cake tins with discs of baking parchment. In a bowl, whisk the egg whites until they are fairly stiff then whisk in the caster sugar, a spoonful at a time. When the sugar is all incorporated, fold in the cooled pistachios. Divide the meringue between the tins, leaving a margin around the edges, and smooth the tops. Bake in the slow oven (top left oven in a 4-door Aga) for 2½–3 hours. Take the tins out of the oven and let them cool enough for you to tip out the meringues and peel off the baking parchment – this is easiest done while the meringues are still warm.

To make the filling, whip the cream until it forms soft peaks, then whisk in the orange juice, followed by the icing sugar and vanilla. Then fold in the orange zest – if you whisk it in, it sticks around the whisk and takes ages to pick it off. Put a small blob of filling on a serving plate to anchor the cake. Put a meringue disc on this, cover with the orange and vanilla cream, and top with the other meringue.

To serve, dust lightly with icing sugar and slice with a serrated knife.

Iced cappuccino parfait

with toasted marshmallow meringue

An irresistible pudding that freezes well for up to 6 weeks – if you manage not to eat it! The marshmallow meringue can be whisked up and left for 2 hours before you spoon it over the parfaits and toast it with a blowtorch.

Serves 6

2 large egg whites
3 oz/75 g sieved icing sugar
¾ pint/450 ml double cream
1 tsp coffee essence
¼ tsp powdered cinnamon

2 large egg whites
6 oz/175 g sieved icing sugar
a little caster sugar

for the marshmallow meringue

To make the parfaits, line 6 ramekins with clingfilm. Whisk the egg whites until they are fairly stiff, then whisk in the icing sugar, a spoonful at a time. When it is all incorporated cover the bowl with a plate. Then, using the same whisk – no need to wash it, providing you whisk in this order – beat the double cream with the coffee essence and cinnamon until it is thick. Fold together the two mixtures and divide between the ramekins. Cover and freeze them.

For the marshmallow meringue, whisk the egg whites in a bowl over a saucepan of simmering water. When they are frothy but not yet stiff, whisk in the icing sugar. Continue to whisk, over the heat, and the mixture will thicken and increase in volume by about half as much again. Take the bowl off the heat, and continue to whisk until the bowl cools slightly. When it is cold cover it with a plate.

. . . .

To serve, turn out each parfait on to a plate – do this just before you start the meal and put them into the fridge. Just before serving spoon over each parfait some of the marshmallow meringue, dust with a little caster sugar, and run the blowtorch over them until the exterior is lightly toasted.

Blueberry tart

with lemon and toasted almond pastry

These tastes go together beautifully. I particularly love cooked blueberries – their taste is sharper than when they are raw and they need sugar – or honey, if you prefer: a tablespoon per ounce (25 g) of sugar. Serve the tart with crème fraiche or whipped cream.

Serves 6

for the meringue
4 oz/110 g butter, hard from the fridge, diced
5 oz/150 g plain flour
2 rounded tbsp icing sugar
finely grated zest of 1 lemon
2 oz/50 g flaked almonds, dry-fried

for the filling
1½ lb/675 g blueberries
4 tbsp cold water
4 oz/110 g granulated sugar, or more to taste
2 rounded tsp arrowroot, mixed with 1 tbsp water

To make the pastry, put the butter, flour, icing sugar and lemon zest into a food-processor and whiz until you have fine crumbs. Tip them into a 9-in/22-cm flan dish, and add the toasted flaked almonds. With your fingers, incorporate them with the pastry crumbs, then press the mixture firmly around the sides and base of the dish. Put it into the fridge for at least 1 hour. Bake in a preheated moderate oven, 350°F/180°C/Gas Mark 4 (bottom right oven in a 4-door Aga), for 15–20 minutes, or until the pastry is just coming away from the sides of the dish. If it has slipped down the sides, press it back up with a metal spoon and return it to the oven for a couple of minutes. Take it out and let it cool.

To make the filling, put the blueberries into a saucepan with the water, cover the pan with its lid, and cook gently over a moderate heat until the juices run and the berries are very soft. Then add the sugar, and stir until it has dissolved. Mix some of the hot juice with the arrowroot mixture, then stir it into the contents of the pan, until the berries and their juices are bubbling. Take the pan off the heat, let it cool, then pour the contents into the cooled baked pastry shell.

Rich lemon curd shortbread

This is enough for 8 greedy people, or 12 conservative eaters. The lemon curd can be made a week ahead, and the finished shortbread can be cooled and kept in an airtight container in the fridge for 3–4 days.

Serves 8

1 large whole egg   *for the lemon curd*
2 large egg yolks
5 oz/150 g caster sugar
4 oz/110 g butter, diced
finely grated zest and juice of 2 lemons

6 oz/175 g semolina   *for the shortbread*
6 oz/175 g plain flour
6 oz/175 g golden granulated sugar
8 oz/225 g butter, hard from the fridge, diced
a few drops of liquid vanilla extract
finely grated zest of 1 lemon

Beat together the eggs and yolks in a Pyrex bowl, then stir in the rest of the lemon curd ingredients. Put the bowl over a saucepan of simmering water, and cook until the sugar dissolves, the butter melts, and the curd thickens. There is no need to stir continually, just from time to time. When the curd is very thick, take the bowl off the heat and leave it to cool.

To make the shortbread, put the semolina, flour and sugar into a food-processor with the butter. Whiz until the mixture resembles fine crumbs. Whiz in the vanilla and lemon zest. Press the mixture firmly down into an oblong baking tray, approximately 10 x 14 in/ 25 x 35 cm, and put it into the fridge for 1 hour. Bake in a preheated moderate oven, 350°F/180°C/Gas Mark 4 (bottom right oven in a 4-door Aga), for 20 minutes, when the shortbread should be biscuit-coloured and just shrinking away from the sides of the tray. Take it out of the oven, spread over the lemon curd, and bake for a further 5 minutes at the same temperature. Take it out and let it cool a little. Cut it into squares or fingers while it is still warm.

Dark chocolate cappuccino mousse cake

Chocolate with coffee again, but this time in a rich cake with a soft, creamy top. If you like – and I do – serve the cake with a warm caramel sauce: see page 260. You can make the cake a day in advance – keep the tin covered with clingfilm.

Serves 6

for the base

4 oz/110 g dark chocolate
4 large eggs, separated
4 oz/110 g caster sugar
a pinch of salt

for the cappuccino mousse

2 tsp best-quality instant coffee granules
3 tbsp boiling water
½ sachet powdered gelatine, soaked in 1 tbsp cold water, *or*
** 2 leaves gelatine, soaked in cold water**
3 large egg whites
3 oz/75 g icing sugar, sieved
½ pint/300 ml double cream
4 oz/110 g dark chocolate

Preheat the oven to 350°F/180°C/Gas Mark 4.

To make the base, line a 9 in/22 cm springform cake tin with a disc of baking parchment. Break the chocolate into a bowl and set it over a saucepan containing barely simmering water – don't let the base touch the water. Let it melt and then cool a little. Whisk the egg yolks with the caster sugar until they are pale and very thick. Then stir the melted, slightly cooled chocolate thoroughly into the egg mixture. In another bowl, using a scrupulously clean whisk, beat the egg whites with the salt until they are stiff. Then, with a large metal spoon, fold them quickly and thoroughly through the chocolate mixture. Pour and scrape this into the lined cake tin, and bake in the moderate oven (bottom right oven in a 4-door Aga) for 25 minutes, or until when you press the centre it feels springy. Let it cool in the tin, then carefully turn it out, peel off the paper and replace the cake in the tin.

To make the mousse, dissolve the coffee granules in the boiling water, then immediately dissolve the gelatine in it. (The leaf gelatine dissolves almost instantly as it is lifted from its cold water and dropped into the heat of the coffee. The soaked powdered gelatine needs stirring.) Leave to cool completely. Continue in the following order and you won't need to wash the whisk until you have finished. Whisk the egg whites with a pinch of salt until they are fairly stiff, then add the icing sugar, a little at a time, whisking continuously until all the sugar is incorporated. Cover the bowl with a plate. Whip the cream until it holds soft peaks, then fold in the cooled coffee mixture. With a large metal spoon, fold the egg white mixture into the coffee cream. Pour this over the chocolate cake base. Smooth it even, and give the cake tin a couple of thumps on a work surface, to dislodge any air bubbles. Leave it to set.

. . . .

To serve, release the spring to loosen the sides of the cake and lift out the mousse cake, on the tin base, and put it on a serving plate. Hold the block of dark chocolate in a double thickness of foil, and, using a potato peeler, shave curls off it. Scatter them over the surface and around the base of the mousse cake.

Rich dark chocolate and almond cake

with chocolate cream

The cake element of this recipe appears in my book Sweet Things, *written many years ago. It is still the best rich chocolate cake I know – and I have tried many, many recipes – and even knocks spots off the famous Austrian Sachertorte – the only thing about Austrian cooking that I've encountered which disappoints. This is a convenient pudding-type cake, and intensely satisfying for chocolate lovers. But it will only be as good as the chocolate you use in it. It improves if it is made 3 days in advance; it can be covered with the chocolate cream several hours before serving.*

Serves 6

6 oz/175 g dark chocolate
6 oz/175 g butter
6 oz/175 g caster sugar
3 large eggs
6 oz/175 g ground almonds, sieved
one of the following:
½ tsp liquid *or* powdered vanilla extract, *or* the finely grated zest of 1 orange,
**   *or* 2 tsp coffee essence**

for the
chocolate cream
6 oz/175 g dark chocolate
¼ pint/l50 ml double cream

To make the cake, preheat the oven to 325°F/170°C/Gas Mark 3.

Put a disc of baking parchment in the base of a non-stick 8-inch/20-cm cake tin. Break up the chocolate into a heatproof bowl and put it over a saucepan of barely simmering water – do not let the base of the bowl touch the water. Let it melt, then take the bowl off the heat. Put the butter into another bowl and beat it, gradually adding the sugar, until it is pale and fluffy. Beat in the eggs, one by one, and the ground almonds alternately with them. Beat in your chosen flavouring and, lastly, the cooled melted chocolate. Pour and scrape this mixture into the lined cake tin, and bake in the low to moderate oven (bottom of the bottom right oven in a 4-door Aga), for about 45 minutes. Take it out of the oven, let it cool in the tin, then turn it out on to a serving plate.

To make the chocolate cream, break the chocolate into a saucepan, pour in the cream and set it over a very gentle heat. As the chocolate melts, stir it into the cream. Take the pan off the heat.

Use a palette knife to spread the chocolate cream over the entire cake, top and sides, getting it as smooth as you would like it. It will become thick and glossy as it cools.

Bûche de Noël

Serves 6

This makes a splendid alternative to Christmas Pudding and can conveniently be made 2–3 days ahead. It is sheer indulgence for those who, like me, are passionate about chocolate.

8 large eggs, separated
8 oz/225 g caster sugar
8 oz/225 g dark chocolate
a pinch of salt

for the filling and covering

8 oz/225 g dark chocolate
1 pint/600 ml double cream
4 oz/110 g white chocolate
a spoonful of icing sugar

Preheat the oven to 350°F/180°C/Gas Mark 4.

Line a 12 x 16 in/30 x 40 cm baking tray with baking parchment; put a dab of butter in the corners to anchor the paper. Whisk the egg yolks with the caster sugar until they are pale and very thick. Then break the chocolate into a bowl, and put it over a saucepan of barely simmering water – take care that the base of the bowl does not touch the water. When the chocolate has melted, lift it from the saucepan, and let it cool for several minutes. Then scrape it into the yolks mixture, and stir thoroughly. In a clean bowl and with a scrupulously clean whisk, whisk up the egg whites with the salt until they are very stiff. With a large metal spoon, fold the whites thoroughly through the chocolate mixture. Scrape this on to the prepared lined baking tray, smoothing it evenly, and bake in the moderate oven (bottom right oven in a 4-door Aga), for 20 minutes. Take it out of the oven, cover it with a very slightly damp cloth and leave to cool.

Make the filling/covering: put the dark chocolate, broken-up, into a saucepan with ½ pint/300 ml of the cream, and let the chocolate melt over a moderate heat. Then stir it into the cream – at first it will look curdled, but don't worry, as you stir it all comes together. Let it cool. Meanwhile, whip the rest of the cream until it stands in soft peaks. Fold it into the cooled chocolate cream.

Break the white chocolate into a bowl, and let it melt very, very gently over a pan of hot water. Take great care not to let the bottom of the bowl touch the water – white chocolate needs even greater caution when being melted than dark chocolate.

To assemble the *bûche*, lay a sheet of baking parchment on a work surface. Tip the cake on to this, and carefully peel off the paper. Spread about a third of the chocolate cream over it, and roll it up lengthways. Cut off a diagonal slice about a third of the way down the length, and stick it on to the side, to give the effect of a small branch. Put the *bûche* on to a serving plate, and spread over it the rest of the chocolate cream. With a fork, swirl the melted white chocolate over the ends. Make patterns down the 'bark' – the dark chocolate covering – with a fork.

NB If the *bûche* cracks as you roll it up, don't worry: mould it, with your hands, in the paper, to a rounder shape. It is quite malleable.

. . . .

Sieve over the icing sugar just before serving, to give a lightly snowed-on effect.

Dark chocolate and vanilla banana cream pie

I made this first when I had a quantity of Vanilla Bavarian Cream left over. I sliced the bananas and put them under the heaped-up cream, so that they would not discolour. The chocolate pastry base can be baked up to a week ahead, providing that you store it in a thick polythene bag. The custard mixture can be made a couple of days in advance, and the whole pie assembled several hours before serving – in the morning for supper or dinner that evening.

Serves 6

6 bananas

for the
pastry base

4 oz/110 g butter, hard from the fridge, diced
5 oz/125 g plain flour
1 oz/25 g icing sugar
1 tbsp cocoa powder – *not* drinking chocolate
a few drops vanilla extract *or* a shake of powdered vanilla extract

for the vanilla
custard cream

1 pint/600 ml single cream
1 split vanilla pod *or* ½ tsp powdered vanilla extract
6 large egg yolks
4 oz/110 g caster sugar
2 leaves Costa gelatine, soaked in cold water, *or* 2 tsp powdered gelatine,
**   soaked in 3 tbsp cold water**
½ pint double cream, whipped

Put the pastry ingredients into a food processor and whiz to the texture of fine crumbs. Press them firmly around the sides and base of a 9-in/22-cm flan dish or tin. Put it into the fridge for at least 1 hour. Bake in a preheated moderate oven, 350°F/180°C/Gas Mark 4 (bottom right oven in a 4-door Aga), for 20–25 minutes, until the pastry is beginning to shrink away from the sides of the dish. If it slips down, press it back up with a metal spoon and put it back into the oven for a couple of minutes.

To make the custard cream, put the single cream into a saucepan with the vanilla, over a moderate heat, until the cream is very hot but not boiling. Take it off, and leave it until it is cold. Then scrape the tiny black seeds from the split vanilla pod into the cream, remove the pod, and reheat the cream gently. Meanwhile, beat together the egg yolks and sugar, then pour in the hot vanilla cream and mix very well. Cook the custard in a microwave oven for 1 minute on high, then stir the contents of the bowl briskly with a balloon whisk; cook again for 30 seconds on medium, then take it out and stir. Continue to cook, on medium for 30 seconds at a time, until the custard has thickened. Otherwise put the bowl over a saucepan of simmering water and stir the custard until it thickens, about 40–45 minutes. Be warned: you don't think it will thicken, but it will. When the custard has thickened stir in the leaves of gelatine (minus the water they have soaked in) or the sponged-up powdered gelatine, until it has dissolved completely. Leave the custard to cool. When it is beginning to set fold it into the whipped cream.

· ·

To assemble the pie, peel and slice the bananas over the rich chocolate pastry base, and pile the vanilla cream over them. If you like – lily-gilding, this – scatter grated dark chocolate over the surface. Yum.

Dark chocolate ginger biscuits

The perfect ending to a simple lunch or supper with a cup of coffee or tea.
They will keep in an airtight container for 3–5 days.

4 oz/110 g butter
2 oz/50 g caster sugar
4 oz/110 g self-raising flour
2 rounded tsp ground ginger
8 oz/225 g dark chocolate

Preheat the oven to 350°F/180°C/Gas Mark 4. Beat together the butter and sugar until the mixture is light and fluffy. Sieve in the flour and ground ginger, a little at a time, beating until it is all incorporated and you have a stiff dough. Take pieces of dough about the size of a walnut and roll them into balls between your palms – if your hands become sticky, dust them with flour. Put the dough balls on a baking tray (no need to butter or oil it), spaced well apart, and flatten them with a fork. Bake in the moderate oven (bottom right oven in a 4-door Aga) for 10–15 minutes, or until the biscuits are light golden brown. They will feel softish, but they firm up as they cool. Leave them on the baking tray for a minute or two once they are out of the oven, then lift them off with a palette knife and leave them to cool on a wire rack.

Break the chocolate into a bowl, and put it over a saucepan of barely simmering water – do not let the bottom of the pan touch the water. Let the chocolate melt. Then dip half of each biscuit in the melted chocolate and put them to set on a plastic tray, or a tray lined with a sheet of baking parchment. When cold, store them in an airtight container.

Rich pecan and dark chocolate biscuits

These biscuits make a good pudding substitute, at the end of supper or lunch with a cup of coffee. They will keep in an airtight tin for 3–5 days.

8 oz/225 g plain flour
8 oz/225 g butter, hard from the fridge, diced
4 oz/110 g soft brown sugar
½ tsp liquid vanilla extract, *or* **½ tsp powdered vanilla extract**
6 oz/175 g pecan nuts, dry-fried, then roughly chopped

6 oz/175 g best-quality – minimum 70% cocoa solids – dark chocolate *for the coating*
2 oz/50 g butter

Put the flour, butter, sugar and vanilla into a food-processor and whiz to a crumb-like texture. Then add the chopped nuts and whiz them briefly into the crumbs. Tip the mixture on to a floured work surface, and knead it quickly to a dough. Press or roll it out, then cut out 12 biscuits with a 2-in/5-cm scone-cutter. Put them – I use a palette knife – on to a baking tray and leave it in the fridge for 1 hour. Bake in a preheated moderate oven, 350°F/180°C/Gas Mark 4 (bottom right oven in a 4-door Aga), for about 15 minutes. Take the biscuits out, leave them for a couple of minutes on the baking tray, then carefully, with a palette knife, lift them on to a wire cooling rack.

To make the coating, put the chocolate and butter into a bowl over a saucepan of simmering water, and stir as they melt. Let the bowl cool for 5 minutes, then spread each biscuit thickly with the chocolate mixture. The butter content helps prevent the chocolate assume a dull, matt appearance as it sets. When they are cold, store the biscuits in an airtight container, with a sheet of baking parchment between the layers.

Marrons glacés and maple syrup semi-freddo

A delicious half-way house between a cream and an ice cream. Again it has to be made in advance so that it has time to freeze, but take it into room temperature at the start of the meal so that it reaches the correct consistency before you serve it. If you can get thin chestnut honey, pour a spoonful over each semi-freddo before you serve it. If you like, serve them with crisp almond biscuits or vanilla shortbread.

Serves 6

4 tbsp maple syrup
3 egg yolks
1 egg white
a pinch of salt
6 marrons glacés, finely chopped
½ pint/300 ml double cream, whipped to soft peaks

Line 6 ramekins with clingfilm.

Measure the maple syrup into a saucepan and warm it over a moderate heat until it is very hot. Whisk the egg yolks, then continue to whisk as you pour in the very hot syrup from the saucepan. Whisk until the mixture is very pale and thick – this takes several minutes. Then with a clean whisk, beat the egg white with a tiny pinch of salt. Fold the chopped marrons into the whipped cream, then the maple syrup mixture and, lastly, the egg whites. Divide it between the 6 lined ramekins, and bang each twice on the work surface to remove any air pockets. Cover with clingfilm, and freeze.

. . . .

To serve, bring the ramekins out of the freezer and into room temperature for 1 hour. Then turn out on to individual plates and peel off the clingfilm.

Pecan caramel vanilla ice cream

I like to eat ice cream all year round but in the winter months I serve it with a warm sauce. Try this nutty ice cream with a warm dark chocolate sauce (see page 259) or a caramel one from page 260. The ice cream will freeze well for up to 6 weeks, and you can make the caramel a couple of days before you put together the ice – store it in an airtight container.

Serves 6

6 oz/175 g granulated sugar
3 oz/75 g pecans, chopped, dry-fried for several minutes and cooled
3 large egg whites
a pinch of salt
3 oz/75 g icing sugar, sieved
½ pint/300 ml double cream
½ tsp liquid vanilla extract *or* ½ tsp powder vanilla extract

Butter a baking tray. Put the granulated sugar into a heavy-bottomed saucepan over a moderate heat. Shake the pan until the granules begin to dissolve around the edges. *Don't stir it and don't try to hurry it.* When the sugar is a molten caramel, tip in the pecans and cook over a low heat for a minute, shaking, then pour the pecan caramel on to the baking tray and leave it to cool. When it is cold, cover the caramel with a sheet of baking parchment and bash it into chunks.

To make the ice cream, whisk the egg whites with the salt until they are stiff. Then, whisking continuously, add the icing sugar. With the same whisk, whip the cream, adding the vanilla as you go, until it holds soft peaks. Fold the egg whites into the cream then fold in the pecan caramel chips. Pour the ice cream into a suitable container and freeze.

. . . .

To serve, take the ice cream out of the freezer and put it into the fridge before you start the meal. After the first course, bring it into room temperature while you have the main course to let it soften a little.

Baked ice cream meringue

This is really Baked Alaska without the sponge. Much as I love Baked Alaska, the ice cream and hot meringue, I don't like the semi-frozen sponge base. We leave it out of this version, and I think it is much improved by its absence. And this is a wonderful pudding for using up leftover egg whites. Freeze the whole meringue-covered ice cream for up to 2 weeks in an ovenproof dish so that you can bake it before serving.

Serves 6

for the
ice cream
3 egg whites
pinch of salt
3 oz/75 g icing sugar, sieved
½ pint/300 ml double cream
½ tsp liquid vanilla extract *or* ½ tsp powdered vanilla extract

for the
meringue
4 large egg whites
a pinch of salt
6 oz/175 g icing sugar, sieved

to finish
1 tbsp granulated sugar
4 tbsp brandy, optional

If you make the ice cream in the order that follows there is no need to wash the whisk until you have finished. Whisk the egg whites with a pinch of salt until stiff, then, whisking all the time, add the icing sugar. Cover the bowl with a plate, then whip the cream, adding the vanilla. With a large metal spoon fold together the egg whites into the cream mixture, spoon it into an ovenproof dish and freeze.

For the meringue, whisk the egg whites with a pinch of salt until fairly stiff. Then whisk in the icing sugar until the meringue is stiff and glossy. Pile the meringue over the frozen ice cream in its ovenproof dish, and refreeze.

The iced pudding keeps in the freezer for up to 5 weeks.

To finish, take the dish out of the freezer and put it into the fridge as you start the meal. Scatter the granulated sugar over the surface and bake in a preheated moderate oven, 350°F/180°C/Gas Mark 4 (bottom right oven in a 4-door Aga), for 10 minutes. Meanwhile, if you are using the brandy, warm it in a small saucepan. Take the baked ice-cream meringue out of the oven and put it on the work surface. Light a match, ignite the warmed brandy in its pan, and pour it, flaming, over the meringue. Serve immediately.

You could, instead of baking this iced pudding, take it out of the freezer and, after 5 minutes at room temperature, scatter the sugar over the surface. Take a blowtorch and, holding it no closer than 12 inches/30 cm so that the meringue does not burn, caramelize the sugar on the surface. Then flame it with brandy – or not, as you choose.

Iced lime, almond and vanilla bombe

Anything 'iced' is convenient because it has to be made sufficiently far in advance for it to freeze. You can prepare this bombe in a bowl, in the traditional bombe shape, or, as I prefer, in a terrine or long dish, which is easier to slice and serve. I always line the dish or terrine with clingfilm, which makes it easy to turn out. It will freeze well for up to 6 weeks. To chop crystallized fruit, dip the knife in hot water from time to time to get rid of the stickiness.

Serves 6

8 oz/225 g best assorted crystallized fruits, chopped
finely grated zest of 3 limes and juice of 2
3 oz/75 g flaked almonds, dry-fried then cooled
½ pint/300 ml double cream, whipped to soft peaks
3 egg whites
3 oz/75 g icing sugar, sieved

Fold the chopped crystallized fruits, lime zest and juice, and the almonds into the whipped cream. Cover the bowl and put it into the fridge. Put the egg whites into a bowl over a saucepan of gently simmering water, and whisk. When they are frothy, whisk in the icing sugar, and continue to whisk until the meringue is very stiff. Take the bowl off the heat, and whisk until it feels cool. Then, with a large metal spoon, fold the meringue into the fruit and nut mixture. Line a loaf tin or terrine with clingfilm, carefully pushing it into the corners, and fill it with the ice-cream mixture. Bang the tin or dish several times on a work surface to remove any air pockets, cover it with clingfilm, and freeze.

. . . .

Turn the bombe out before you sit down to eat: take off the covering clingfilm, tip it on to a serving plate, peel off the clingfilm. Leave it in the fridge until you are ready for it, then slice it thickly.

Redcurrant and lemon water ice

The perfect light, refreshing conclusion to an otherwise rich lunch or dinner.
You can freeze it for up to 6 weeks.   **Serves 6**

1 pint/600 ml water
8 oz/225 g granulated sugar
pared rind and juice of 2 lemons (well washed first)
1 lb/450 g redcurrants, stripped off their stalks

Put the water, sugar and lemon rind (not yet the juice) into a heavy-bottomed saucepan over a moderate heat. Stir until the sugar dissolves completely, then boil for 5 minutes. Take the pan off the heat, and add the lemon juice and the redcurrants. Leave it to cool, then liquidize and sieve the fruity syrup – to get rid of the tiny woody seeds. Freeze the purée in a solid polythene container. When it is frozen, chip out the contents into a food-processor and whiz until smooth, then refreeze. Repeat this process 4 times. Each time you do it, the ice will become smoother, greater in volume, and easier to spoon out of the container.

. . . .

Serve it straight from the freezer.

Extras and

essentials

This chapter contains some recipes that don't readily fit any-where else but they are all useful. Not all are for eating – during my Christmas-decoration demonstrations I am often asked how to dry sliced citrus fruit, so I have included the instruc-tions on page 269. You will also find recipes for Mayonnaise (page 250) and Vinaigrette (page 251). They taste as I like them, but taste is an individual thing: if you like your vinaigrette sharper than mine, add more wine vinegar. Similarly, purists wouldn't include sugar in their mayonnaise, but I think it's a vital ingredient. And I love Dijon mustard in my mayonnaise, but others may well prefer English. So cook as you like to eat. The recipes are the guidelines, and you can adjust them accordingly.

Some of these recipes are for nibbles to eat with drinks – Pumpkin Seeds (page 257), for example, and Spiced Pecans on page 256. Both can be made a couple of days in advance, keep well in screw-topped jars, and are infinitely nicer to eat than bought peanuts or crisps.

The Christmas Cake recipe isn't my usual one but I made it in 2001, wanting a change from almond paste, white icing and a dark fruit cake. I revived an old recipe of mine for a blond cake, made sev-eral amendments to the original and the result is on page 262.

This chapter contains much that is crucial to my many cooking demonstrations.

Mayonnaise

The only decent mayonnaise in the UK is home-made. It is impossible to buy good commercially made mayonnaise. When you read the ingredients on the labels you will easily understand why. Mayonnaise is effortless to make – the only chore is washing up the food-processor afterwards – and it is so good with hot food as well as cold. You can add an immense variety of seasonings to a basic mayonnaise to enhance whatever it is to be served with – for instance, try finely chopped dill and diced cucumber, skinned and seeded, with all grilled, baked or barbecued fish. A little medium-strength curry powder, and honey instead of sugar in the basic recipe, is very good with smoked chicken and mango, or with deep-fried mushrooms in a light batter. And I'd eat mayonnaise spiked with my favourite chilli and garlic with almost anything! Home-made mayonnaise will keep for up to 4 days in the fridge.

Serves 6

1 large egg
1 large egg yolk
1 tsp caster sugar
½ tsp salt
a very good grinding of black pepper
2 tsp best-quality Dijon mustard
½ pint/300ml olive oil
juice of 1 lemon
2 tbsp white wine vinegar

Put the egg, the yolk, the sugar, salt, pepper and Dijon mustard into a food-processor. Whiz, then tip the food-processor as you continue to whiz, adding the olive oil drop by drop. Once you have an emulsion, you can put the food-processor flat on the surface and pour in the olive oil, whizzing, in a thin, steady trickle. When it is all incorporated, whiz in the lemon juice and wine vinegar. Taste, and add more vinegar if you like a sharper taste. If the mayonnaise is too thick, whiz in a tablespoon or two of near-boiling water.

Scrape the mayonnaise with a plastic spatula into a bowl or wide-necked jar, cover, and store it in the fridge.

Vinaigrette

Tastes vary so much when it comes to vinaigrette (or French dressing, which is the same thing). This is my basic recipe, to which you can add finely chopped fresh herbs, or finely grated lime or lemon zest or finely chopped anchovies and capers – very good with vegetables and fish: spoon it over when they are still hot so that they absorb the dressing's flavours. Store the basic vinaigrette in a screw-topped jar and use as needed.

1 tsp salt
1 tsp freshly ground black pepper
1 tsp caster sugar
½ tsp English mustard powder
¼ pint/150 ml best olive oil
2 tbsp white *or* red wine vinegar

Put the ingredients into a clean jar, screw on the lid and shake vigorously before using.

Hollandaise sauce

This is such an easy recipe and the basis for a selection of variations to complement a wide range of dishes, fish, meat, chicken or vegetable. In its basic form hollandaise will dress up smoked haddock or hot smoked-salmon fishcakes, asparagus, purple-sprouting broccoli or globe artichokes. It can transform any simple risotto into a luxury dish, and, of course, it is one of the star players in Eggs Benedict. It is a myth that hollandaise needs to be made at the last minute; you can keep it warm for an hour before you need it – but not over direct heat or it will curdle. If it shows the slightest sign of doing so, whisk it like mad, or add a spoonful or two of cream and whisk it in.

Serves 6

3 large egg yolks
8 oz/225 g butter, diced
2 tbsp reduced, flavoured wine vinegar (see below)

Fill a saucepan with water to a third full and put it on to boil. When it reaches a gentle simmer, put over it a bowl containing the beaten egg yolks, and, with a balloon whisk, add the butter a little at a time. When all the butter is incorporated you should have a thick, glossy sauce that closely resembles a good custard. Whisk in the reduced wine vinegar and take the bowl off the heat. It will keep warm for up to an hour – whisk in any thin skin that forms.

Variations: add chopped mint, which turns hollandaise into sauce Paloise. It is excellent with lamb in any form – roast leg, rack, or grilled lamb chops.

Add skinned and diced tomatoes and chopped dill to serve it with fish, particularly baked salmon.

Add chopped tarragon, snipped chives and the jelly from beneath a roast and it becomes sauce Béarnaise, good with any meat but particularly beef.

To reduce wine vinegar

1 bottle white wine vinegar
1 onion, skinned and quartered
2 bay leaves
2 tsp black peppercorns
a few celery leaves
2–3 crushed parsley stalks

Put everything into a pan and simmer until the vinegar has reduced by half. This gives a much greater depth of flavour to a Hollandaise Sauce than merely sharpening it with lemon juice. Cool, strain and discard the contents of the sieve. Store the reduced flavoured vinegar in a screw-topped jar, and use as required. It keeps in the fridge indefinitely.

Stock

Nothing makes a better soup than good stock. Chicken stock is my staple, and I freeze it in plastic mineral-water bottles – somehow, in cylindrical form, it takes up negligible space in a freezer, unlike a bowl-shaped container. Stock substitutes are a must for the storecupboard, though. We can't all always have stock to hand. The three I buy are all additive free, and the additive they are chiefly free from is monosodium glutamate. They are Kallo, in cube form, Marigold, in powdered form, and Benedicta, which is a liquid.

2 roast chicken carcasses, *or* 1 fresh uncooked carcass
3 onions, with skin, halved
2 carrots, washed and chopped into 3 chunks
2 leeks, washed and chopped into 3–4 chunks
celery leaves, and the washed base of the celery
3 tsp black peppercorns
2–3 bay leaves
a handful of crushed parsley stalks – crushing them releases the flavour
2 tsp salt

Put all of the ingredients into a large saucepan and cover with cold water. Bring it to the boil, then cover the pan with its lid, and cook in a slow oven, 250°F/125°C/Gas Mark ½, for at least 6 hours, or overnight is preferable. Now, if you have an Aga, this is easy. I cook stock in the top left oven of my 4-door Aga, and always overnight. But I would buy a plug-in slow cooker for items such as stock (oxtail and ham hocks are other items which need very lengthy cooking time). Let the stock cool, strain it, and, once it is cold, freeze it, or store it in the fridge for 3 days, providing that it will be simmered for at least 15 minutes in the soup or sauce-making process.

extras and essentials

Caper and anchovy butter

Delicious with fish or grilled steak. It can be made 2 days in advance. If you find anchovy fillets too salty, soak them in milk for 1 hour and pat them dry on kitchen paper before you chop them. If at all possible, buy capers preserved in olive oil – usually found in health-food shops. If you cannot find them, buy salted, rinse them well in a sieve under running cold water, then marinate them, too, in milk to reduce their saltiness. They are infinitely nicer than capers preserved in brine.

Serves 6

8 oz/225g butter, softened
6 anchovy fillets, drained and very finely chopped
2 tsp best-quality capers, preserved in oil, finely chopped
1 tsp sweet paprika pepper
a good grinding of black pepper

Put the butter into a bowl and beat in the other ingredients thoroughly. Lay a sheet of baking parchment on a work surface, and pile on to it the caper and anchovy butter. Work the butter into a fat sausage shape on the paper, and roll the paper around it. Put the roll into the fridge. Before serving, unwrap it and cut it into even slices.

Spiced pecans

Very good with drinks – make more than you think you'll need. They'll disappear. They can be stored in an airtight container for a couple of days. So much nicer than crisps or peanuts.

4 tbsp olive oil
½ tsp salt
2 tsp Worcester sauce
1 scant tsp Tabasco
8 oz/225 g pecan halves

Heat the oil in a non-stick sauté pan with the salt, Worcester sauce and Tabasco. Add the pecans, and stir from time to time over a moderate heat for 15–20 minutes. The nuts will brown as they cook in the spicy oil. Then with a slotted spoon, lift them on to a wide dish containing a couple of thicknesses of absorbent kitchen paper to soak up the excess oil and leave them to cool.

Pumpkin seeds

At Hallowe'en, when pumpkins are at their peak, don't throw away the seeds. They are delicious fried, and extremely nutritious. They must be dried thoroughly before you fry them. Once dried, you can store them in screw-topped jars and then fry them several hours before serving them with drinks. Pull any stringy orange fibres off the seeds and rinse them well in a large sieve under running water. Pat them dry with kitchen paper, then spread them out on a large baking sheet and leave them in an airing cupboard, or somewhere else consistently warm, for several days, until they are crisp. Let them cool, then store them in a screw-topped jar until you want to fry them. Outside pumpkin season you can buy seeds from health-food shops.

3 tbsp olive oil
1 tsp salt
½ tsp medium-strength curry powder
½ tsp cumin seeds, bashed in a mortar with a pestle or with the end of a rolling pin
6 oz/175 g dried pumpkin seeds

Heat the olive oil, salt, curry powder and crushed cumin in a non-stick sauté pan. Let the spices and salt cook for a minute in the hot oil then add the pumpkin seeds. Stir them, over a moderate heat, for 10 minutes, then scoop them on to a couple of thicknesses of kitchen paper to cool. Serve them on the day they are fried.

Basic crêpe batter

When I began to make crêpes – more years ago now than I want to calculate – I decided to make them more interesting than just adding salt and pepper or sugar to the batter and began to flavour it according to the proposed filling: for instance, I whizzed in a quantity of mixed herbs – snipped chives, flat-leaf parsley, chervil and some dill for a fish filling, or finely grated lemon zest and vanilla with strawberries and cream. Orange zest went into the batter for my version of Crêpes Suzette, and cinnamon pancakes are lovely with an apple and raisin filling. Really, the choice is endless. Here is the recipe for a basic batter. It is essential to use whole milk, never even semi-skimmed, for crêpe batters. It makes 12 crêpes.

Serves 6

4 oz/110 g plain flour
2 large eggs
½ pint/300 ml full-fat milk

Put all of the above ingredients into a blender and whiz until smooth. Pour the batter into a jug, and leave it to stand for at least 30 minutes before you make the crêpes. Flavour it according to the crêpes' future filling.

Chocolate sauce

The best version I have ever come across. It keeps well in the fridge for up to a week – it will almost solidify, but it becomes pourable again when warmed gently. You can make it a week in advance.

6 oz/175 g soft light brown sugar

2 level tbsp cocoa – I like Green and Black's best (absolutely *not* drinking chocolate, ever, in place of the cocoa)

3 oz/75 g butter

3 tbsp golden syrup – dip the spoon in very hot water before spooning the syrup so that the syrup slips off easily

½ pint/300 ml near-boiling water

½ tsp liquid *or* powdered vanilla extract

Put all of the ingredients into a saucepan over a moderate heat. Stir until the butter has melted and the sugar dissolved, then boil quite fast for 3–4 minutes. Cool, and pour the sauce into either a screw-topped jar or a jug and cover it with clingfilm. Once the sauce has cooled completely, store in the fridge. You can then gently warm up the jug and its contents before serving.

Caramel sauces

Here are two versions of this most useful sauce – which could just as well be called butterscotch sauce. In the first version, when the sauce is cold and stored in the fridge, it separates, but don't worry: on reheating and stirring it comes together again. Don't do what one friend did and skim off the buttery top! In both cases, this amount is enough for 6 people, served over vanilla ice cream, or coffee or chocolate ice cream. Yum.

Caramel sauce made with butter

½ pint/300 ml water
6 oz/175 g granulated sugar
2 oz/50 g Demerara sugar
8 oz/225 g butter, diced
½ tsp liquid *or* powdered vanilla extract

Put the water and both sugars into a saucepan over a moderate heat and shake the pan gently until the sugar has dissolved. Only then, when the sugars are dissolved, can you let the liquid come to the boil. Boil fast for 10 minutes. Take the pan off the heat and whisk in the butter, a little at a time, then whisk in the vanilla. Let it cool, and store it in a screw-topped jar in the fridge.

Caramel sauce made with cream

½ pint/300 ml cold water
6 oz/175 g granulated sugar
2 oz/50 g Demerara sugar
½ pint/300 ml double cream
½ tsp liquid *or* powdered vanilla extract

Put the water and the sugars into a saucepan over a moderate heat and shake the pan gently until the sugar has dissolved. Then boil fast for 10 minutes. Take the pan off the heat, add the cream and vanilla and stir for a further 2–3 minutes. The sauce will thicken. Let it cool and store it in a screw-topped jar in the fridge.

Christmas cake – with a difference

After thirty-two years of marriage I heeded Godfrey's plaintive cry that he doesn't like marzipan – and how about making a Christmas cake without it? In 2002 he will have his wish! My cake, rich and dense in texture, is in the freezer, and I intend to thaw it over 48 hours before I finish its top with a simple arrangement of nuts and dried fruit. A large red ribbon tied around it will complete it. Out of the freezer, it will keep for 2–3 weeks.

1½ lb/675 g best-quality raisins, Lexia if possible
4 oz/110 g preserved ginger, chopped
4 oz/110 g best-quality candied lemon and orange peel, chopped
8 oz/225 g crystallized pineapple, rinsed, chopped and dried
8 oz/225 g dried – semi-dried are the best – apricots, snipped small
2 oz/50 g dried blueberries or cranberries
4 oz/110 g plain flour
12 oz/350 g butter
12 oz/350 g soft light brown sugar
8 large eggs
4 large egg yolks
8 oz/225 g ground almonds, sieved
finely grated zest of 1 orange
finely grated zest of 1 lemon
¼ pint/150 ml brandy
½ tsp almond extract

for the pecan halves
decoration apricot jam
crystallized fruit, e.g. pears and apricots, each sliced thinly

Preheat the oven to 300°F/150°C/Gas Mark 2.

Butter a 10-in/25-cm deep cake tin, dust it out with flour and line the sides and base with baking parchment.

In a large bowl mix together all the fruits. Sieve the flour over them and then, with your hands, mix the fruit and flour together so that each bit of fruit is coated in flour.

extras and essentials

In a large bowl beat together the butter and soft light brown sugar until the mixture is pale and fluffy. In a smaller bowl beat the eggs with the yolks, then beat them, a little at a time, into the butter mixture, alternating with the ground almonds. Then, with a large wooden spoon, stir in the floured fruit and the orange and lemon zest very thoroughly. Lastly, mix in the brandy and the almond extract. Pour the contents of your mixing bowl into the prepared cake tin, and smooth the top even, then hollow it slightly in the middle. Put a disc of baking parchment on the top. Bake in the low moderate oven (bottom of the bottom right oven in a 4-door Aga) for 1¼–1¾ hours. Push a knife into the centre – if it comes out sticky, bake for a further 20 minutes before testing again. Let the cake cool in its tin. When it is completely cold, take it out of the tin, wrap it first in greaseproof paper then in foil, and freeze it. Thaw for 48 hours, the week before Christmas.

To decorate, warm the apricot jam in a saucepan, and brush it over the surface of the cake. Arrange the pecan nuts and the thinly sliced fruit as you choose, and in the quantities you prefer. Tie a wide red satin ribbon around the cake for a Christmassy effect.

Dark chocolate truffles

with Angostura bitters

Way back when Godfrey and I married, he was a very good cook. These days, it takes a bit of effort to remember him at the stove, but I know he really did make cheese soufflé – it isn't a figment of my imagination! One of the things he taught me was to put Angostura bitters into rich, dark chocolate truffles. You can make them up to a week before you eat them – or give them away as a present.

**1 lb/450 g best-quality dark chocolate, broken up
(I like Green and Black's Organic dark chocolate)
1 tsp best-quality instant coffee granules
1 tbsp boiling water
¼ tsp liquid *or* powdered vanilla extract
8 oz/225 g butter
about 6 drops of Angostura bitters
cocoa, to roll the truffles in**

Making truffles, in the final stages, is messy, so be prepared!

Put the chocolate into a Pyrex or similar bowl. Dissolve the coffee in the water with the vanilla and add it to the chocolate. Put the bowl over a saucepan containing barely simmering water – don't let the bottom of the bowl touch the water. Warm the bowl until the chocolate has melted, but take great care not to overheat it. Then take the bowl off the heat, and beat in the butter, a little at a time. Then beat in the Angostura bitters. Put the bowl in a cool place – ideally, a larder – for the mixture to cool and firm up. Later, sieve some cocoa on to a large plate. Rub some onto your hands, which should be as cool as possible. Scoop teaspoons of the chocolate truffle mixture into your palms, and roll them into balls then in the plate of cocoa to coat them. You should end up with about 24. Put the truffles into a box or tin as they are made, and store them, once finished, in the fridge.

Kinloch fudge

We make this fudge nearly every day to serve with coffee after dinner each evening. We are endlessly asked for the recipe, so here it is. I have to thank Katharine Robertson, who worked here with us for many years, for the original. Whenever I think of her I always see her stirring the fudge! This makes a full 9 x 12 inch/22 x 30 cm baking tray.

8 oz/225 g butter
2 lb/900 g granulated sugar
1 tin condensed milk
the empty tin filled with full cream milk
½ tsp liquid *or* powdered vanilla extract

Butter the baking tray.

Put all of the ingredients into a large saucepan over a moderate heat. Stir until the butter has melted and the sugar completely dissolved. *Don't let it boil before the sugar has dissolved* – before the sugar has dissolved, you can feel a gritty sensation under your wooden spoon as you stir. Then, boil the fudge – beware, it will rise up the sides of the saucepan. Stir, and when it becomes fudge-coloured from its original very light colour, drip a tiny amount into a bowl of cold water. If it forms a soft ball, it is ready. Take the pan off the heat, and stir quite vigorously until the fudge thickens and cools a bit, about 7 minutes. Pour and scrape the thick fudge into the baking tray. Leave it to cool, then cut it into squares. When it is cold, lift out the squares with a palette knife and store them in an airtight tin until you want to eat them.

For chocolate fudge, mix 2 tablespoons sieved cocoa powder with the granulated sugar before you put the sugar into the pan at the start of the fudge-making session – it will mix in, though at first you will wonder.

Marmalade

Everyone likes their marmalade different. I love ours, but I also love other people's as a change. Nothing beats the first marmalade of the season, and, with this recipe, every making tastes just slightly different, according to the balance of citrus fruit used. The only chore is scrubbing the fruit before simmering it. Your house fills with its clean, fresh smell. I prefer to boil it up in single batches – getting a set is quicker, which gives a bright fresh colour and flavour to the marmalade. Which is how I like it.

**Makes
10 lb/5 kg**

**3 lb/1.35 kg citrus fruit, half in Seville oranges, the rest in lemons,
limes, pink grapefruit, sweet oranges or clementines
6 lb/2.7 kg granulated *or* preserving sugar**

Have ready 10–12 1-lb/450-g jars, each scrupulously clean.

Scrub each fruit well under running hot water, then put them all into a large saucepan. Add 4 pints/2.4 litres of cold water. Bring the water in the pan to a simmer then cover it with its lid, and continue to simmer for 6 hours. The lid must fit closely, to prevent too much liquid evaporating from the pan. When the fruit is quite soft when stuck with a fork, let the pan and its contents cool. Lift out each fruit on to a board, and cut it in half. Scoop the pips and the flesh into a smaller saucepan. Don't discard the water. Add 1 pint/600 ml of water to the pips and fruit flesh, and simmer for 20 minutes over a moderate heat. Let it cool, and strain it into the water in the large saucepan.

Meanwhile, slice or chop the cooked fruit shells, whichever you like, and return the peel to the large saucepan. Add the sugar, turn on the heat and stir until the sugar has dissolved. When you can no longer feel any grittiness beneath your wooden spoon, allow the marmalade to come to the boil, then let it boil fast – a rolling boil. It needs careful watching because it will rise right up the sides of the pan. Let it boil like this for 15 minutes, stirring occasionally. If it comes near the top of the pan, blow on it hard to reduce the volume of the boil – overboiled marmalade smells vile! After 15 minutes' fast boiling, carefully pull the pan off the heat, drip some marmalade on to a chilled saucer and leave it for several minutes. Then push the surface gently with your fingertip: if it wrinkles, you have a set. If it is still runny, put the pan back on to the heat, bring it back to a fast boil for 5 minutes, then repeat the test. Take care always to pull the pan off the heat when you test for a set. (I've discovered that, somehow, getting a set is nigh on impossible if you use a non-stick pan for making marmalade.) When you have a set, warm the jars and pot the marmalade – I use a jug. Cover each with a waxed disc, and seal with Cellophane. When they are cold, label the jars, date them, and store them in a cool place.

Pickled lemons, limes or Seville oranges

I learned how to pickle lemons from Clarissa Dickson-Wright many years ago. It is so easy, and they are so useful that I always have a large Kilner jarful in the larder or, once opened, in the fridge. I use them chiefly in long, slow-cooked lamb shank recipes, but they are very good cooked with anything that contains lentils, too. The fruit should be packed into the jar as tightly as possible.

Scrub the fruit under running hot water. Then quarter each piece lengthwise, but do not cut right through the base. Put each nearly quartered lemon (or lime or orange) into the jar, and push a tablespoon of flaky salt into it – inevitably some will spill out, which is why it is best to do this in the jar. When you have crammed in as much fruit as possible, boil the kettle and fill the jar to the surface with water. Seal it. Leave the jar and its contents unopened for at least 4 weeks. Once opened, it will keep in the fridge for a year. Chop or slice the fruit thinly before using them.

extras and essentials

Dried sliced citrus fruit

This is a recipe for non-edible Christmas decorations! It was several years ago that I first saw sliced oranges among Christmas decorations, but it seemed impossible to buy them. I decided to dry my own. I soon discovered how easy it is to dry them too quickly, thereby browning the skins and ruining the appearance. On the plus side I also discovered that lemons, clementines and limes can be dried too, just as successfully as oranges. They take 4 days to dry out, in warmth but not direct heat.

Because you aren't going to eat the sliced fruit there is no need to scrub it before you slice it. Use a really sharp serrated knife to slice it as thinly as possible. Put it on to wire mesh cake-cooling racks in an airing cupboard – put a tea-towel over any clothes underneath the racks. If you have an Aga, arrange the racks on the cooling plate at the side of the cooking plates. Be prepared to move them when you need to use the hob. In the absence of an airing cupboard or Aga, leave the racks of sliced fruit in a warm room until the interior of each slice is truly dried out. Don't be tempted to put them in the oven at even the coolest setting – the bright, fresh colour of the outer peel will vanish. Buy wire from a florist, wire the slices in pairs or as you like, and stick them among any greenery. Throw them away after you take down your decorations. They won't keep their colour for another Christmas.

Index

Valued suppliers

So much food can be bought by telephone or via the internet these days that I thought the details of a few of our trusted suppliers might be helpful. After all, the very best of all foods is grown (fruit, vegetables), raised (meat, game), caught (fish and shellfish), and made or preserved (smoked fish, jams, relishes and honey) in the Highlands and Islands of Scotland – one of the last wilderness areas in Europe.

John Gilbertson, Isle of Skye Seafoods
Broadford, Isle of Skye
01471 822135
www.skye-seafood.co.uk
I've already mentioned his wonderful seafood in several recipes here.

Duncan Fraser, our excellent butcher in Inverness
01463 233066
For the best sausages in the world, and excellent white puddings too.

Salar, South Uist
01870 610324
www.salar.co.uk
They hot-smoke the best salmon, and call it 'flaky' smoked salmon.

Valvona & Crolla, Elm Row, Edinburgh
0131 556 6066
www.valvonacrolla.co.uk
For all the best...that comes from Italy!

The Gourmet's Lair, Inverness
01463 225151
www.gourmetslair.co.uk
This is where we buy all our cheeses and much else in the delicatessen line.

Irvine Robertson Wines, Leith
0131 553 3521
www.irvinerobertson.co.uk
For the best service, and wines to match.

Sleepy Hollow Smokehouse, Aultbea, Ross-shire
01445 731304
For the most delicious smoked salmon and other smoked delicacies.

Summer Isles Foods at the Achiltibuie Smokehouse, Ross-shire
01854 622353
For smoked salmon and wonderful smoked chicken breasts.